Rebecca Wachter
060 E 450 N APT 110
Provo Utah 84601   8-1-84

The Osmonds
A Family Biography

The Osmonds
A Family Biography

MARSHA DALY

St. Martin's Press
New York

THE OSMONDS: A FAMILY BIOGRAPHY. Copyright © 1983 by Marsha Daly. All rights reserved. Printed in the United States of America. No part of this book may be used or reproduced in any manner whatsoever without written permission except in the case of brief quotations embodied in critical articles or reviews. For information, address St. Martin's Press, 175 Fifth Avenue, New York, N.Y. 10010.

Library of Congress Cataloging in Publication Data

Daly, Marsha.
　The Osmonds : a family biography.

　Includes index.
　1. Osmonds (Musical group)　2. Musicians—United States—Biography.　I. Title.
ML421083D3　1983　　784.5'4'00922　[B]　　83-9636
ISBN 0-312-58944-1

First Edition

10　9　8　7　6　5　4　3　2　1

To RL, ever patient, ever understanding

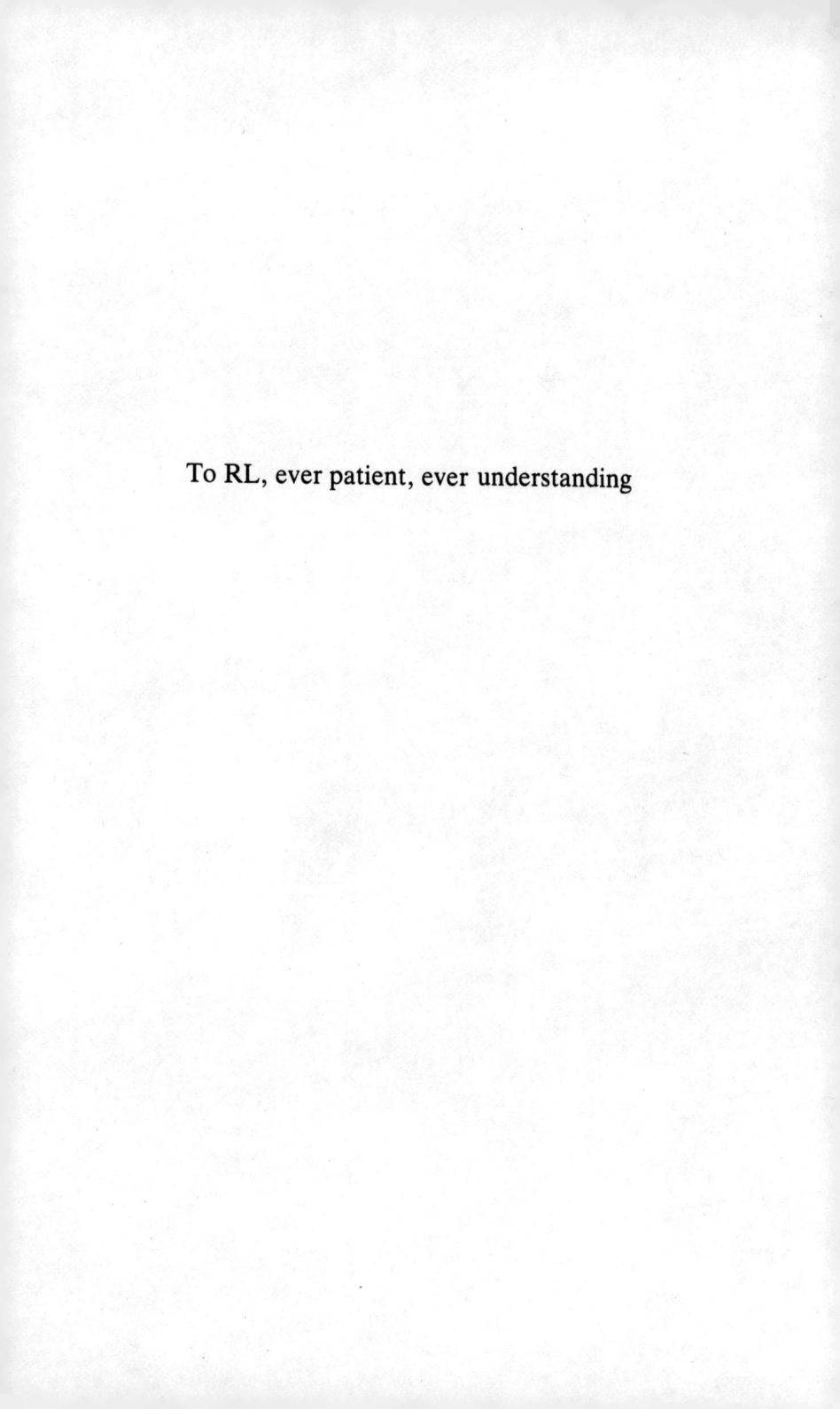

CONTENTS

	Introduction	ix
1.	The Osmonds of Ogden	1
2.	Westward Ho Osmonds!	18
3.	Osmondmania	31
4.	A Little Bit Country, A Little Bit Rock 'n' Roll	49
5.	Marie Makes a Big Mistake	80
6.	Marie Spreads Her Wings	88
7.	Donny Gives His Regards to Broadway	98
8.	A Secret Love	107
9.	Marie's Wedding Day	114
10.	Still Singing After All These Years	120
	Appendix: Vital statistics of each Osmond	133

A section of photographs follows page 48.

INTRODUCTION

When they run out onstage with their flashy, million-dollar smiles, the seven singing Osmonds make it all look so easy, as if any like-minded family could do the same. That may be their secret weapon, the ability to be all things to all people. Looking at them, Alan, Wayne, Merrill, Jay, Donny, Marie, and Jimmy Osmond seem to lead charmed lives. The Osmonds have been in show business for over twenty-five years and they have had the successes, fame, and fortune most entertainers can only dream about. That should make them as happy as those professional smiles they flash indicate they are.

Upon close examination of their lives, however, one finds an edge of sadness to the family, most notably to Donny and Marie, the superstars of the family. Behind the sugary, happy image the Osmonds skillfully created for their public, they seem to have had their fair share of sorrow, heartache, and bad times.

Why else would a grown-up Donny admit: "In a way, it would have been nice to live a normal life. . . . Show business has been good to me. However, I want my children to lead as normal a life as possible." And Marie more than once has wistfully said, "I had to sacrifice a lot. I grew up in a suitcase. I never did the things normal girls do. I missed out on a lot of happy times."

And yet, both are still entertainers, looking for a success to equal their teen stardom. But that is really just part of the enigma that makes this family so fascinating.

The fact is that the Osmonds, even at the height of their

success, never fit into the show business fraternity. When their career brought them to Hollywood, the entertainment mecca of the world, they kept their main home in Utah, a state most record and TV moguls would have trouble finding on the map.

In the '70s, the era of violence, heavy drugs, cynicism, and hard-driving rock in the record industry, they became superstars as devout Mormons. As such, they are forbidden to smoke, drink alcohol, use drugs, or drink anything with caffeine, which includes all colas, tea, and coffee. They are also forbidden to engage in premarital or adulterous sex.

These beliefs saw them branded as "dull" and "goody-goodies," and made them objects of derision for many of their fellow performers, not to mention important television and music critics, as if a family that placed such high value on virtue could not be exciting entertainers. Despite the obstacles, the Osmonds had the last laugh, outlasting most of the entertainers who got cheap laughs at their expense. The Osmonds have done so through a shrewd ability to switch gears and latch on to new forms of popular music.

How the family rose to superstardom and have managed to stay there is a story of faith and courage. Some might say there was an element of luck in it, but wiser people know that the successful make their own luck. And, as their story unfolds, it will be obvious that the Osmonds made success happen.

From their humble beginnings in the mountains of Utah, through their TV and record hits, the Osmonds have been the embodiment of the American spirit. As Mormons, they believe that success and prosperity are sure signs of God's love, that he favors his chosen people with the good life. If this is so, the Osmonds truly are God's favored!

But there has been a price the family has paid, both emotional and physical. Olive Osmond, the mother of the clan, proudly claims that none of the children was ever compelled to perform, that it all happened quite naturally. Even as children, she says, they seemed to "thrive on challenges. When we had just a singing act in the beginning, they thought they'd never make it as a recording or nightclub act, but they tried and succeeded. The next challenge was doing concerts, and that attracted crowds, too." Beyond the pure joy they got from entertaining, Olive adds that her children "believe they're on a mission, using the challenge that God gave them."

And it is true that the Osmonds in their "mission" have given more to life than they have taken. But then, they believe, as Olive says, that "Our life is God's gift to us, and what we do with it is our own gift to him."

That may be why the Osmonds have driven themselves to the brink of exhaustion, have ignored illness and personal needs to bring their message to the world through song. Professionally, it has worked. Today, around the world, millions regard this act as America's First Family of Song.

Their story is very inspirational and at times sad. But, if for no other reason, it is worth telling because they prove that old-fashioned values—hard work, discipline, and respect for elders are as meaningful today as ever. They have not just mouthed their beliefs, they have lived them every day of their lives. To understand what makes the Osmonds so different, it is important to learn their family motto: "No matter what decisions you make, no matter what you do, it is always family first, religion second, and business third."

1

The Osmonds of Ogden

The American West has always been a breeding ground for rugged individualism. Its wide open spaces and sparse population demand that its inhabitants be independent to survive. The Osmonds are proud to be a part of the West and its tradition. No matter to what exotic or remote places their careers have taken them, the Osmonds always feel a strong pull back to their roots in Utah with its scenic mountains and fertile valleys.

But Utah is more than that to the Osmonds. It is the cradle of their religious order, the Church of Jesus Christ of Latter Day Saints, more commonly referred to as Mormonism. When Brigham Young led his disciples into the mountainous region, Utah was just a U.S. territory (statehood would not come until 1896). The Mormons were a small set of Christians whose practice of polygamy had made them outcasts in whatever American cities they had settled in, as the more widely held morals dictated one wife for each man.

In 1847, Young and his followers established their claims in the unsettled federal territory. Most of the other pioneers were bound for California, and when at last others began to notice Utah, the Mormons were firmly in control. After Utah entered statehood most Mormons gave up polygamy but little else. Through the ensuing decades their network of successful businesses and their growing numbers in the area insured control over the state's political structure. It is the one place where Mormons feel completely safe to practice their rigid and secretive religion without fear of public scorn.

To see why the Osmonds have been so successful, it is necessary to understand the basic tenets of Mormonism. While the family comes first, everything revolves around the church. Mormons believe that they have been given the word of God through ancient elders and there is life after death with a final judgement day when all will be brought before God to answer for their earthly lives. That is why they remain pure of alcohol, tobacco, stimulants, or even the thought of illicit sex. Considering the ultraliberated life style of most of the other states, it is no wonder Mormons are so clannish, clustering in Utah where their children are not exposed to outside forces.

In the 1940s, of course, it was much easier to keep children blindly faithful, as television had not brought new, free, and sophisticated concepts into everybody's home. Before TV, most folks were born, raised, and lived their lives pretty close to their families.

Olive Davis, a bright, articulate, and extremely vivacious girl, probably never seriously believed she would leave her home in Utah. As a child, she cherished dreams of being a fashion designer, which would have taken her to one of the big cities. But World War II began, forcing her to put aside girlish dreams for more practical notions. Ever practical, Olive had taken bookkeeping and secretarial courses in school so she would always be able to support herself—not that she expected to actually do so, but the skills would also be useful to a husband.

It was in 1944, while she was working in the military supply depot near Ogden, Utah, that George Osmond walked into Olive's life. It was a day she would never forget. Olive, like all the other young women, had met plenty of nice young eligible soldiers while she worked on the base, but she sensed something different about George.

Most girls wonder if they will ever find "Mr. Right," but

Olive seems to have known instinctively that it was her destiny to be joined forever to a man with whom she could raise a large, happy, close-knit family. Much later, Olive would admit that the day she met George, she wrote in her diary that she thought he was the man she would marry.

George was quite taken with the teenager, too. He had recently been discharged from the army, due to a bad ulcer, and liked Olive enough to stay around to take her out. It began casually with picnics, long walks, and local dances. George, eight years older than eighteen-year-old Olive, talked honestly about his prospects. He could return to his father's farm in Star Valley, Wyoming, where he had been raised, or he could stay in Utah and marry Olive.

When he asked her to marry him, Olive had her doubts. It was the biggest step she would ever take, and she wasn't sure what life with George Osmond would be like. He had little to offer except the desire to work hard and provide a good life for his family, but his ambition was in his favor.

Olive liked the way he talked about his childhood, of the love and respect he felt working side by side with his dad on the farm. There was a sense of sharing, of belonging, by taking on his load of responsibility around the farm. Having to work hard had not made George bitter or angry toward his father, but taught him to respect what his parents had done for him. Those farm years shaped George's own value system. He learned there are "darn few problems between parents and children when they are working together, each contributing to a common goal. That is what I wanted for my children."

That deep commitment to a family life was shared by Olive. She was raised to believe that the "family is the important central unit in the Mormon religion. And I think when children think a family is forever, it makes them feel secure."

Whatever doubts still lingered about marrying George faded away after a private talk Olive had with her mother. She reminded Olive that her husband, Olive's dad, was a poor man when she had married him; all he had had to offer was "a log cabin in Idaho," but they had enjoyed a good, solid marriage. Love was what held two people together, not money.

Less than a year after that first meeting, Olive became Mrs. George Osmond, and a dynasty was about to begin. The young couple put their roots down in Ogden, where George set up his own insurance business. That first year was a real struggle. Like all newlyweds, their relationship was sometimes shaky. Olive discovered that George expected her to be a traditional housewife while she, strong-willed and independent, thought of herself as an equal partner in their union. She worked side by side with George in his business enterprises, handling his secretarial work and bookkeeping. And yet, he expected her to also handle all the usual house chores.

Both admit that they had some loud, bitter battles that first year. Without that strong commitment to their "for-all-eternity" vows, the couple might have split.

Many years later, Olive admitted to her only daughter, Marie, how more than once she was tempted "to throw in the towel," but managed to hold her tongue and ride out the disagreement. And, she told Marie, as she and George matured, they grew more tolerant of each other. They learned to work together as a good, strong team.

Both Osmonds were ambitious. Besides the insurance business, Olive studied real estate, passed her test and became a licensed realtor. If a boom came to Ogden, they were ready to cash in on it.

They were settling into a good routine when Olive had the best news of all. She was pregnant. From then on, their plans revolved around building a good life not just for themselves but for the baby and the many children they expected would follow.

Their main interest was in investing any extra cash. They lived frugally and began to buy up real estate. Property, if handled well, is an excellent long-term money-making investment. And its true worth is beyond money, as it can provide enough food to feed one's own family as well as shelter. The Osmonds knew that real estate could make them not only prosperous but self-sufficient.

The expected baby made the couple newly aware of their

blessings. Olive was delighted when her neighbors surprised her with a baby shower. Olive has said, "I had the name Marie picked out before I had any of the children"—and most of her friends brought her dainty, feminine baby clothes. But when the newest Osmond made his appearance in the world, somehow the gifts did not suit him and they were carefully packed away for another baby. They named their firstborn son George Virl Jr., and he seemed a perfect baby.

As he developed, however, Olive noticed that he did not respond to their voices like other children might. She was about to have her second baby by the time they had Virl, as they called him, examined by an ear specialist. Olive was shattered to learn that Virl had a severe hearing problem. He was legally deaf, with no hearing in one ear and only twenty-five percent hearing in the other.

Devastated, Olive realized the hardships Virl would face. Deaf children in the '40s were paid little attention in the schools. Often they were shunted into institutions, taught minimal job skills, and forgotten by the hearing world. Virl was only two when Olive decided that he would not be abandoned by his family, even if she had to teach him herself!

Concerned for her second son, Tom, the couple took him for hearing tests. Once again, they heard the terrible news. Not only was Tom also impaired, but his was a worse condition than Virl's; he had virtually no hearing in either ear.

Such news has defeated many families. Wives and husbands too often carry guilt inside of them, blaming each other for any imperfection when their children are less than perfect. But their sons' handicap served to unite George and Olive behind a common cause—to give their sons a normal life.

Deep inside, of course, Olive had nagging fears about expanding the family. Virl and Tom were very dear to her, but sometimes their needs were overwhelming. Family and friends thought they were helping by advising the couple that it would be in the boys' best interests to be sent to an institution where they would have friends that shared their handicap.

The Osmonds wrestled endlessly with their options. Fortunately, they had their strong faith to guide them in making difficult choices. In the end, Olive decided to raise the boys at home where she could personally supervise their education. It has been said that of sight, sound, and voice, the worst loss is hearing, because those who have never heard voices or sounds really lose both senses. Deaf children in Virl and Tom's time were taught sign language and to lip read, but were not encouraged to develop their vocal cords.

Olive learned all she could about deafness. Not much research was available on teaching the deaf to speak, but, instinctively, she knew that if she could get the boys to use their vocal chords, they would develop normally and eventually learn to speak. Olive bought records of sounds and had the boys try to imitate those words. With time and patience, Olive succeeded, and years later her methods were the same used by speech specialists in many schools.

Neither parent loved the boys less because of their handicap. If anything, it made them more protective, and they had to guard against a natural tendency to be overly careful. But they also had to be realistic about their situation.

There were others in their family similarly afflicted with hearing deficiencies, which seemed to indicate that it was hereditary. Any other child they bore would run the risk of being deaf, too. Did it make sense, they wondered, to even consider having another child? They could not fool themselves about the cost of raising Virl and Tom. Ahead of them were special schools and expensive medical assistance. Even without taking into account the expense, was it fair to the child to take such a risk knowing the odds?

It was a time of great soul searching for the Osmonds. At times, Olive got very discouraged. Was her dream of a big, boisterous family laughing and working together to end? Luckily, Olive was plucky; her dreams died hard. They resolved to accept what God gave them.

No doubt Olive was worried throughout her next pregnancy. If the situation occurred today, she could take an easy test for women who have a history of problem pregnancies to detect any genetic defects of babies while they are still in the womb. But all Olive and George could do in 1949 was wait and pray.

Alan Ralph was born on June 22, 1949. Again, he was a healthy looking baby and this time, George and Olive were elated because he was truly perfect. Their prayers had been answered. That news made Olive's next pregnancy much easier. Olive was still hoping to name the little one Marie, but somehow Wayne Melvin sounded better for the baby. He arrived on August 28, 1951.

If Olive was disappointed in mothering a brood of boys, she never let on. They could be a mischievous handful but as soon as they could walk, the Osmonds gave them simple tasks that used up some of their boundless energy.

Because of the way the family was expanding, the Osmonds had bought a farm in Ogden, a place where the boys could be raised in the healthy outdoors and learn the value of work. George was a hard taskmaster and a strict disciplinarian who believed that children should learn right from wrong at a very early age. Olive was the one they ran to for comfort, although she never interfered with George's rules.

The discipline, of course, was meted out with love. "You have to give them guidance when they are young," George says, "so that this becomes a habit when they are older. I have always been a strict father—you have to be, with nine children—and they have all had a spanking if they needed it."

The house rule was "Father is not always right, but he is always Father." And the respect they were taught to give him has never changed—even after they were grown up and had families of their own. Merrill has said about his relationship with his father, "I can't remember a time when any of us bucked his advice on an important matter."

Responsibility comes naturally to farm families. At times an extra pair of tiny untrained hands can be a nuisance, but George and Olive realized that you are never too young to learn good work habits, and with practice, the boys became adept at feeding the chickens, gathering eggs, pitching hay, and caring for the horses and cattle.

They raised most of their own food on the farm, so adding to the family was not a burden. Merrill Davis was welcomed into the family on April 30, 1953, followed on March 2, 1955, by Jay Wesley. A seventh son was born in the early morning hours of December 9, 1957, leading some to believe that perhaps the ancient myth about seventh sons is true—they are supposed to be born under lucky stars. Indeed, their seventh son, Donald Clark, grew up to be the most successful of the bunch. As a teen idol, Donny would earn the many millions of dollars that turned the Osmonds into one of the richest dynasties in show business. But he was just another of Olive's miraculously healthy sons in 1957.

Olive spent her days bustling around the kitchen like a mother hen. Virl and Tom were old enough to be sent to the Utah School for the Deaf, where they learned how to lip read. (All of the Osmonds also learned sign language, which was the quickest way to communicate with each other.) They were still home most of the time, a part of the family fun. And Olive still devoted part of every day to their speech lessons.

Mormon women consider themselves nurturers, which is why many have large families, and motherhood was a role made for Olive. Just as she taught the children that honest labor is one of God's blessings, so did she encourage them to fill their leisure time. After their chores were done, the boys loved to get up a baseball or football game. After the game came dinner, and after dinner came family time. They would sit and chat for a while playing games like checkers, and discuss the day's events. Or they would start an old-fashioned sing-along. That pleased George and Olive, who were musically inclined. When George was a boy in Wyoming, he had been active in his church choir. Olive was quite accomplished on the saxophone, and as a teenage girl, she had earned pocket money by playing in a dance band. They both still loved to dance and the boys grew up with music.

To keep the boys home as much as possible, the Osmonds tried to make their home as attractive as possible. With their strict religious teachings, they were afraid the lads might be tempted into non-Mormon acts. Olive took charge of family projects, keeping the kids busy and under her watchful eye. For example, one summer they all pitched in to build a lake on the farm. They passed many pleasant summer hours swimming in that lake and the Utah winters were perfect for ice-skating. Each of them felt a certain thrill of accomplishment whenever they were using the lake because of the labor they had contributed. The boys loved the farm because there were trees to climb, horses to ride, and swings. It was a great big private playground. But music was becoming the underlying force in their lives.

At first, the music revolved around the church. As soon as each Osmond was old enough to sit still, he was brought for services, sitting with the family, even participating. Mormons do not hold very formal services; instead, each church member is expected to talk and participate in the weekly gathering. Even the children are encouraged to get up on the podium to talk about their thoughts or families or to sing a song. The adults are as mindful of these contributions as they are of older members'. Olive attributes her family's show business success to these services, in that they helped bring her children out of their "private shells" and gave them ease in dealing with large groups. Mormons believe in modesty but frown upon shyness.

Between school and church, Olive's brood had little time to get into trouble. But they were still quite small. It was usually older boys who wanted independence and Olive worried about that happening with her own. In any town there is always a group of unsupervised boys hanging out on street corners, sneaking smokes, experimenting with whiskey and sex, and Provo was no exception. Olive searched for ways to hold her family together.

Again, it was her church that offered the answer. The Osmonds all agree that "church is not something we just do on Sundays," but a presence seven days a week. Early on, their home was filled with books by, for, and about Mormonism. And they were not there just to fill up shelf space; Olive studied them in her spare time.

One day she came across an idea in one of the books that would alter the course of the Osmonds' lives. It was a passage explaining how to maintain a stable, happy, family relationship. Olive felt as though the writer were directing the message right at her.

In large families, it is often easy for the older children to ignore the younger and to go their separate ways. Olive wanted a family activity that would involve everyone equally, regardless of age. And there, in "one of the church books," she read how "one of the old prophets had suggested families have one night a week devoted to themselves."

Many Mormon families devote Monday night to sitting down and discussing where they came from and how much they mean to each other, as well as their mutual problems, and plan future events together. They may leaf through the "Book of Remembrance" that each Mormon family is expected to keep up, a book continued from generation to generation with photos of all the relatives. Thus, children gradually learn their history and develop a sense of family pride. Then, too, it is another way to show how Mormon elders are honored by each succeeding generation.

Setting aside one night a week just for the family captured Olive's imagination. But she preferred Friday because the kids could relax more without having to worry about homework or school the next day. That simple decision to initiate a weekly celebration led to the birth of an entertainment dynasty in America!

It began without fanfare. The Osmonds explained to the children that one night a week belonged exclusively to them from now on. Friday night would be "Family Night," and it proved to be an instant hit with the kids.

First, Olive would fix "dinner by candlelight. The kids would tear home from school for this party. And after dinner, the entertainment would be the kids performing. They'd practice all week, learning their music to have a different song to sing or a different tune to play. I guess that's where their music began, way back when they were toddlers."

But, at first, it wasn't the boys' singing that made Family Night a roaring success with Olive; it was watching the boys grow closer to one another. In another way, Family Night was the beginning of the Osmond family's circle of wagons that shut the rest of the world out—not that this bothered them.

There was plenty of music around the house for the boys to pick their songs. Within a few weeks, the boys' entertainment segment dominated their every waking moment. They worked hard to be as professional as possible in their presentation. The slick spots demanded that they spend most of their waking moments practicing their intricate harmonies. George and Olive would help them with their individual parts and later, when the boys were upstairs in bed, the couple would often hear the music waft downstairs as Alan, Wayne, Merrill, and Jay continued experimenting with new chords. Neither parent ever complained; they were pleased to learn that their sons were natural musicians.

The group started off with gospels and, as their voices developed, George introduced them to barbershop music and Dixieland. The boys were apt students, and their folks bought an old wire tape recorder to help them learn their parts. Singing in a group requires special training; voices tend to follow the melody, but in a quartet, each member has to sing his own part, either tenor, alto, baritone or bass, with no wavering into someone else's harmony. It is an acquired skill. The Osmond boys picked their parts up easily.

George was proud of his boys, and he allowed them to sing in church for the first time sometime around 1958. The response was wonderful. Upon first sight, the Osmonds may have looked like a novelty act—cute little boys dressed alike trying to sing—but once they raised their voices in song, the audience knew that they were truly talented. Being cute could get the kids in the door; only their ability would get them asked back. The Osmonds were asked to sing again and often.

It did not take long for word about the Osmonds to spread. With Olive's approval and under George's benevolent supervision, the Osmonds became familiar figures at local weddings and church socials. Even the Lions Club in the area requested the Osmonds for their social events. They were Ogden favorites.

Barbershop quartet music was always popular in small towns, and George had always enjoyed such music. Now that he had his own four moppets, he decided that they could make a unique barbershop group. Barbershop singing dates back to the 1890s and subsequently, quartets have worn the traditional garb of that day—starched shirts, pants with suspenders, and mustaches. Four tiny tots similarly decked out were bound to cause a sensation. George seemed a born showman because his production was a sensation indeed. It remained a family affair, and Olive became their costume designer. The boys needed matching stage outfits and, in a town the size of Ogden, it was nearly impossible to find the same shirt in four different sizes, so Olive put her sewing talents to good use and turned out professional-quality outfits for her busy boys.

The boys loved the singing and the traveling. Olive's capable hands took care of costumes, the farm, and their private holdings. In her spare time, she even ran a successful dress shop in Ogden, without once letting the family suffer. Her competence freed George to take the boys to their singing dates.

But while the boys were embarking on what would be their lifetime careers, Olive had other news. Once again she was pregnant. By this, her eighth pregnancy, she was no longer worried about the child's health, but secretly she still hoped that this time her own special dream would come true and she would have her very own daughter to hold in her arms. Most of the time, though, she worried about the boys—feeding them properly, keeping them out of trouble, and making sure they kept up their studies. The music, she made it clear, was not to interfere with their schooling. Olive came from a long line of educators, and she wanted her children to go to college and find careers that interested them.

Birthdays were always special events in the Osmond household. The family was so large that individual personalities could get lost. But a birthday belonged to just one person, and it became his special day. Olive made the child's favorite dinner and baked a cake and fussed about the birthday boy.

George's birthday was October 13. Even though Olive was ready to deliver at any time, she wanted to make the day an event for her husband. What she did not know was that she would give George an extraordinary present on that day—the one gift no one had ever given him. On that fall day in 1959, Olive felt the first familiar stirrings within her body. Alerting George, they drove to the hospital where he watched as the nurses wheeled Olive toward the delivery room, a route she could have taken them on blindfolded. And George took up his standard spot in the waiting room.

The staff, of course, by now expected to see another strapping Osmond boy enter the world. When the doctor announced that it was a girl, the delivery room personnel applauded with delight. They could hardly wait to tell the expectant father.

One of the nurses ran out of the room to tell George the good news. He was totally unprepared to hear that it was a girl. In fact, he was so stunned by the turn of events that he wandered out of the waiting room and right out the hospital door, so that when the doctor went to the waiting room to see for himself the happy expression on the new father's face, George was nowhere in sight. Later, George had only the vaguest recollection of where he had gone that day. All he could remember was taking a long walk to calm himself down. He has always said a baby girl was the best birthday present anyone could have given him, and Marie has always been a source of great joy to him.

When the shock finally wore off, George wanted to make the day more memorable for Olive, too. Olive used to worry about the boys whenever she went to the hospital, so George always brought them to see her the next day. They were too young to actually be allowed into her room, but she always waved to them as they sat in the parking lot waiting for George to come back. But the day after Marie's birth, George really wanted to show his beloved wife his appreciation. He brought the boys as usual, but this time he lined them up underneath Olive's window. As her face appeared above, the boys burst into song, serenading her with "I Want A Girl Just Like The Girl Who Married Dear

Old Dad." Their rousing rendition of that popular old standard brought lots of heads popping out of windows. The whole hospital staff came outside to watch the fun and the boys gained a lot of new fans.

The celebration continued as the couple brought their newest baby home. She was formally named Olive Marie, and, at long last, the lovely layette of frilly dresses Olive had saved over the years from her many showers came out of the closet. All the Osmonds agreed that "Sissy," as they quickly nicknamed their sister, was adorable.

Now that they had a daughter, the Osmond family seemed to be complete. Olive slipped smoothly into her old routines, getting up to make breakfast for the boys and seeing them off to school, or helping George in his various businesses. Weekends, the boys entertained at nearby events or competed in barbershop competitions. They were quite accomplished singers by now, and formidable competitors. But music was still nothing more than a hobby.

Olive's main concern remained the boys' futures. Both she and George had struggled, as their families before them had, and she hoped that the young Osmonds would have an easier time. They lived close to Brigham Young University, the Utah institution run by Mormons, and Olive encouraged all the children to make that their goal.

She structured the kids' days carefully. Mornings began with the family breakfast. There was a prayer and each Osmond was expected to give a brief outline of his plans for the day. (The tradition of the family breakfast held firm even after the boys were grown up and married. Each morning when they were together in Provo or Los Angeles or wherever, the boys would walk over to their parents home or hotel suite to be part of this ritual.) As youngsters, of course, their daily activities consisted of going to school and completing their chores. The morning was never wasted; Olive set aside a portion of the breakfast time for educational skills. According to Marie, when she and the boys "were little children, there was a blackboard near the kitchen table, and while we ate breakfast, my mother would drill us in grammar and arithmetic."

To some, all of this heavy scheduling and daily planning

made the Osmonds look like little programmed robots when they broke into show business. But as George always said, the "guidance" you give children when they are young "becomes a habit when they are older." It was that way with the Osmonds. Years after the Osmonds had become superstars, a photographer was assigned to shoot the family in Provo and returned to say that the assignment had gone well: "[the] Osmonds were very cooperative. They had scheduled time for me to get them all together, but that is all I was allowed to do. There was no shooting them in candids; their day is so well planned, they just don't have time for relaxed moments. They're really incredible. Maybe that's why they get so much done, but they do look tense a lot of the day. I don't think they ever stop working. But they were also a pleasure to work with because they're so professional. After hours, we never saw them."

George and Olive raised them to be motivated and ingrained in them the idea that life is "a gift from God" and squandering one's time is like a sin. They realized that their work habits were hard for outsiders to understand, but they had such strong faith in the righteousness of their way that they never felt compelled to conform to their peers' less taxing schedules. This sense of conviction and personal courage was the result of childhood hardships, the kind of private heartbreak they tried to hide from the world that admired them for their cheerfulness. And the Osmonds always gave the fans what they wanted, which is why they presented just one face to the world—seven bland, cleancut smiles. Never was an outsider allowed to catch them frowning, or worse, shedding a tear.

When their family life comes up in conversation, the Osmonds speak of their closeness in glowing terms, emphasizing their deep affection for one another, playing up the fun times, playing down the glum times. Mention is always made of their two non-performing brothers and they point out that both are important cogs in the Osmond machine, despite what they refer to as hearing problems. Aside from these brief statements, however, Virl and Tom are virtually unknown outside the family. In many ways, that is their choice, as they are content with the peace they have found in Utah, a peace that only came after years of unhappiness and bitterness that stemmed from being the "unknown Osmonds."

This is a period in their lives that the Osmonds find painful to talk about. And it began with Olive's creation, Family Night. For Alan, Wayne, Merrill, Jay and, later, Donny, Marie, and the ninth child to join the clan, Jimmy, those Friday nights were the highlight of the week. But to Virl and Tom, it was just another cruel reminder of their handicap. Watching their brothers sing and dance to great applause from George and Olive was pure agony. What Olive had devised to draw the family closer was turning into a disaster.

Virl and Tom were the Osmonds who did not smile very much. While Olive had surrounded them at the farm with tender loving care and the same values and virtues as their siblings, their lives had been much more difficult than the others. When they reached school age, both boys attended the Utah School for the Deaf, where they were taught to lip read. They also learned sign language, as did all the other Osmonds.

Virl, because he did have minimal hearing in one ear, was fitted for hearing aids. The aids allowed him to enter the regular school system in Provo. Olive was determined to make his life as normal as possible. Virl was not as sure as his mother that this was in his best interests. At school, his life was like a nightmare. His schoolmates refused to accept the odd boy with the plugs in his ears. He was taunted and when he was on the playground, other boys pulled out his aids. It was years before the bitter memory of what he endured was erased from his memory.

At first, it was not too bad because Virl could escape to the farm, a safe spot where he had lots of playmates. Then came Family Night, and even in his own home, he and Tom felt ostracized. Finally, the two oldest boys confided in their parents, and Olive's heart nearly broke when she realized how the weekly funfest must look through their eyes. There was no way they could end the Friday nights without cheating the other children. But Olive had an inspiration. Why not give Virl and Tom saxophone lessons just like the others? Deaf people usually can appreciate music by touching objects that transmit the vibrations or sound waves. Virl and Tom were never good enough to make a band, but they loved being part of the entertainment on Family Night. Later Olive took them for tap dancing lessons, and the whole family showed their appreciation for how hard the two worked on their routines. Olive probably sighed a sigh of relief when the crisis had passed, but there would be more as the Osmond Quartet attained popularity outside their family circle. But there was no crystal ball to tell the Osmonds what was to come from their innocent warbling.

By 1961, Alan, Wayne, Merrill, and Jay were well known within the barbershop music field. Word of a competition to take place in California was passed along to George. It seemed a fine chance to combine their hobby with a family-style vacation. So George and Olive loaded up the van with food and family and they all hit the road for Pasadena.

They had a grand time, stopping for picnics and singing to help pass the long hours on the highway. The trip would be a major turning point in their lives, but on the way out, it was just a fun-filled jaunt. As soon as the contest was over, they planned to get right back to the farm. There was no way they could have known that for them, the road to California was sprinkled with stardust, and very soon they would visit places their neighbors had only heard about in story and song. The Osmonds were heading for an amateur competition; they would come back professionals!

2

Westward Ho Osmonds!

Pasadena, California, home of the Rose Bowl Parade, is one of America's most beautiful cities. Its proximity to Los Angeles makes it an ideal tourist attraction, so the Osmonds could not help but enjoy their trip. Another plus for aspiring entertainers is that with Los Angeles so close, talent scouts often attend amateur productions looking for possible new stars.

Normally, no Hollywood studio would be interested in a barbershop competition, but there was one enormous entertainment organization into which such old-fashioned music fit perfectly: the Walt Disney company. Disney had built its sprawling, super-successful empire by catering to family audiences. While the moral codes covering movies, television, books, and records were loosening, Disney stuck by the old standards, with no loss of revenue. Disney's big specialty, besides churning out a squeaky clean product, was introducing fresh-faced kids in its films and television show. And in the early 1960s, Disney still had its finger firmly on the pulse of its audience, knowing that teenagers identified with the young performers that it presented on the screen. By the '70s, when nudity and sex scenes that left nothing to the imagination swept the screen, Disney's movie and TV profits were in decline, but when the Osmonds arrived for their California visit, the organization was an investor's dream.

Of course, Disney had another ultraprofitable division aside from the movie business—Disneyland, the cleanest, most efficient, and exciting amusement park ever developed. Millions of tourists flocked through its turnstiles every year. Frequently on summer weekends the park got so crowded that they would have to shut down the admission gates by midafternoon. Disneyland was run like a private city, with as many employees as some towns have. The supervisory personnel, of course, were adults, but Disney, who believed that if you gave a youngster a job, you were guiding him toward responsible adulthood, was the biggest employer of young people in southern California. Disney's standards were high and kids who could not live up to them were quickly dismissed. But any honest, hard-working boy or girl could earn pocket money and have good fun at the same time. Age was not as important as good moral character. Comedian Steve Martin started selling guide books at age ten inside Disneyland's gates and it was at the amusement park that he honed his magic act and storytelling routines.

The park, naturally, needed all types of entertainers, which is why the company was ever on the alert for acts that appealed to customers. A barbershop quartet would fit the down-home theme of Disneyland, and when the agent saw four apple-cheeked lads who looked as if they had stepped directly out of a Norman Rockwell painting, he knew he had found something extraordinary.

After the contest, he approached the family with an offer. The Osmonds were adamant about the family returning to Utah to finish the school year, but the agent offered them a summer job at Disneyland singing their close harmonies. Other ambitious entertainers would have jumped at such an offer. It meant steady employment in the heart of show business—Los Angeles—and a chance to make contacts and attract attention. But the Osmonds considered themselves strictly amateurs; singing was a hobby, the farm was their occupation. Perhaps if the offer had come from some other company, the Osmonds would have declined and gone home forever. But Walt Disney and the Osmonds had similar beliefs about the importance of the family and what was acceptable entertainment. Besides, what red-blooded American boy could say no to spending a summer at the world's most popular funland?

The boys knew that the final decision belonged to Olive and George. But in such important matters, the couple always considered the entire family's thoughts before deciding. That evening they had a family meeting. The children were eager to accept and their parents agreed it was a once-in-a-lifetime opportunity. As the farm and their investments were doing well, whatever the boys earned could be banked for their future. When it came time for the vote, it was unanimous; they would take the job.

Donny was a four-and-a-half-year-old tad and Marie barely out of diapers that summer of '62 when the Osmonds loaded up their van again for California. The boys, in their best barbershop finery, spent the summer as roving entertainers. As such, they roamed around the park, stopping now and again to do a few songs where there was a crowd. The days passed swiftly, and the Osmond Quartet found it exhilarating to be singing for pay—not that they saw much of the money. Right from the start, their parents taught them to be both thrifty and fair with each other. Each had an allowance befitting his age and needs, and the rest of their earnings went into the bank to be invested for the benefit of all the children.

Sundays found the Osmonds still going to church. Los Angeles is one of the few cities outside of Utah with a Mormon temple (as opposed to chapels where members in less populated areas pray), and they never missed a week.

The youthful quartet was so popular around Disneyland that before the summer was out, they had also appeared on a "Wonderful World of Disney" television special. As summer drew to an end, they realized how much fun it had been entertaining people and bringing smiles to their faces. And it seemed that Lady Luck was also smiling down on the Osmonds. After their summer run at Disneyland, there seemed nothing else for them to do but return to Ogden with their happy memories. There certainly was not much demand for their singing style, even if that style was popular with whomever happened to hear it. But they did not have agents and other show business-wise types to look out for them. They were, after all, just a farm family with a little talent and some luck.

Their luck ran strong though. Disneyland brought out the rich and famous along with the middle-class tourists, especially in the evening when it turned into a performer's paradise. By day, the rides and stores were packed; but at night, there were spectacular firework displays and a large arena for live entertainment—often record superstars—which made it a popular entertainment area. One evening Andy Williams' father, Jay Williams, was in the park when he overheard the Osmond Quartet. Seeing the four little brothers sent memories flooding back to him. Some twenty years before, there had been another quartet of talented brothers—the Williams Brothers. And the similarities did not end there. Amazingly, the Williams boys—Bob, Don, Dick and baby Andy—had been organized by their dad to sing in their church, which until then had lacked a choir. Just as a talent scout put the Osmonds on the road to a professional career in music, so had a talent scout from a Des Moines radio station discovered the Wall Lake, Iowa, Williams Brothers and hired them for its own show. Andy was then eight years old. Shortly thereafter, the Williams Brothers got the attention of a Chicago station and were hired for the National Barn Dance program. Papa Williams took a pay cut so that he could move his family there and his sons could continue singing. They moved on to Los Angeles just as the war was breaking out, but the quartet was abruptly split when the two oldest boys were drafted.

After the war, the Williams boys teamed up again and were hired by singer/comedienne Kay Thompson as backup for her night club tour. For six years, they toured the top clubs around the world. But Andy's three brothers tired of the travel and wanted to settle down. Andy, of course, continued, first as featured vocalist for Steve Allen's late-night TV show, and then, with a batch of hit records to his credit, as a solo artist. His hit records led to his own TV shows, and when Jay discovered the Osmonds, Andy had just begun his most successful variety hour to date. The show appealed to the same type of audience as Disney movies—families with children who wanted an easy-listening television series the entire family could watch together. Andy offered a blend of popular standards with some of the new soft rock groups the teen audience was buying. Jay Williams thought his four little discoveries would be a refreshing addition to his son's show. All he had to do was convince Andy.

That was not overly difficult. Like the Osmonds, the Williams clan was very tight. One of Andy's brothers was his agent, another handled his business affairs, and the third was his music arranger. He lived within easy distance of his parents and visited them frequently. And they, in turn, came every Friday night to his taping session at which the show was filmed for network viewing. Even if Andy only said "yes" to listening to his dad's latest discovery out of respect, he was smart enough to realize how appealing the four tykes could be to his audience. After all, this was the day of such homespun entertainment as "Bonanza," the Lennon Sisters, Dinah Shore, and the soon-to-come King Family.

Andy liked what he heard enough to offer the Osmonds a minimum of $10,000 a year if they would move to Los Angeles. This was a much more serious move than spending one summer in Disneyland—Williams wanted them to sign a five-year contract. But, with a little hesitation, they agreed; they were hooked on show business. As George would note in years to come, his sons found singing more fun than pitching hay and plowing fields.

Andy introduced the Osmond Brothers on December 20, 1962, as the "youthful barbershop harmony group from Ogden, Utah." They finished their two songs, "I'm a Ding Dong Daddy from Dumas" and "Side by Side" to rousing applause. And fan mail began pouring in. The Osmonds were a solid part of Andy's TV family from then until the show was cancelled in 1967, and they continued with him thereafter whenever he had specials. True, on their second outing, Andy did mangle the introduction a bit, referring to them as the Ogdens from Osmonds, Utah, but he straightened that out, and it did bring a smile to everyone's face.

No matter what he called them, he genuinely liked the family, from George and Olive right down to Marie. In fact, they were favorites with the whole backstage crew. Maybe the backstage area looked a little like kindergarten with the bubbly and irrepressible kids, especially Donny, running around, but they were well behaved and aware that their parents' watchful eyes were on them at all times.

Once the clan was settled in and the quartet was a definite hit, George and Olive looked around at California and concluded that here was another fine investment opportunity. Firm believers in the advantage of owning over renting, they began buying up apartment houses and evaluating other real estate as a safe place for the boys' money.

At the same time, Olive was pretty busy with her own production. On April 16, 1963, she gave birth to the ninth and final little Osmond, James Arthur, who would forevermore be known as little Jimmy.

With the new baby and a hit show, the Osmonds' life should have been serene. But there was a problem, not a new one, just a new variation—Virl and Tom. The whirlwind introduction to the hectic world of television was easy for the other Osmonds; even Donny and Marie helped out behind the scenes. But it all moved so fast, there was little time to fill in the older boys on what was happening. Suddenly there seemed to be no time for signed explanations, let alone careful lip reading sessions. For once, even Olive was at a loss as to how to solve the situation. The boys' careers were moving too fast and she had to care for little Jimmy.

In the 1963–64 TV season, the Osmond Brothers not only continued as regulars on Andy's show, but they made their dramatic debuts as members of a new ABC-TV series, "The Travels of Jaimie McPheeters." Their roles as the

Kissel children, who were with their parents on a wagon bound for California in the 1840s, were not as large as that played by Kurt Russell, who starred as Jamie, the twelve-year-old boy through whose eyes the main story was told each week. But it gave them a taste of what acting was about.

Their best showcase, however, remained Andy's hour and their harmonizing led to a recording contract. Their records reflected the same type of music they did on the show, and had little appeal for the burgeoning teen market then caught up with the Beatles and other rock groups. But they were steady, if not spectacular, recording stars with their main sales to middle-aged Americans who wanted upbeat, gentle music.

That first season with Andy, the Osmonds were still just Alan, Wayne, Merrill, and Jay. Andy talked about the whole family, but just the quartet was actually seen. Backstage, Donny was getting restless. It was obvious that he wanted to sing with his brothers. Often he amused everyone with his antics, mimicking other stars. Finally, one day Andy happened by when the little scamp was imitating him singing "You Are My Sunshine." Donny's routine broke Andy up and he knew it would do the same to his viewers. So on December 10, 1963, Donny made his nationwide professional debut repeating his vocal impression of "You Are My Sunshine" as sung by Andy. America took the newest Osmond to its heart.

The following summer Andy, as usual, took a group out on the road to play concerts and state fairs. Since the Osmond Brothers were under contract to him, and one of the most popular segments of his TV show, he brought them along. During a show in Allentown, Pennsylvania, Andy brought Donny onstage and the little boy was such a crowd-pleaser that Andy asked him to join the show officially. They would never again be called the Osmond Quartet.

Between shows, the brothers put in lots of practice time, not just on their vocals, but with various instruments. They were a well-rounded group musically, but they believed there was always room for improvement.

The only drawback to their escalating career was that they were left with little time for the farm. Whenever they had a few days off, they drove back, just to touch base again with their roots. But through the rest of the '60s, the Osmonds saw more of the rest of the world than they did of Ogden.

The "Jaimie McPheeters" show was not renewed in 1964, but the Osmonds were far from idle. They guested on other variety shows and put together their numbers for Andy's tours, besides preparing material for their albums. It was increasingly difficult for the brothers to find suitable songs, so they usually wrote the numbers themselves, or at least Alan, Wayne, and Merrill did.

Virl and Tom also solved part of their problem by spending more time on the farm. Then, in the mid '60s, the two went off on their two-year stint as missionaries. (Mormons are under an obligation to give up two years of their lives without pay in the service of others. The Church has established its missions around the world, from the jungles of Guatemala to Japan and Hawaii. On these missions they teach people how to help themselves and, in the process, convert as many natives to Mormonism as possible.) Virl and Tom were two of the first deaf Mormons to do missionary work when they left for Canada and two years of teaching deaf children in a remote area. The family was very proud of their efforts and glad for the chance to finance them. For many years, these two brothers were the only Osmonds to serve in this important capacity; the rest were given a special dispensation as the Church considered their singing tours the equal of a mission. Wherever they went, the Osmonds carried the word of the Mormons, and it is believed that by their thoughts, words, and deeds, some 25,000 converts have been brought into the Church of Jesus Christ Latter-Day Saints. The Osmonds were taught that there are many ways of serving the Church. Their way was to lift millions of people's spirits, a rare gift indeed, and by their life style to be positive proof of what it is to be a good practicing Mormon.

Before Andy's show left the air in May of 1967, all of the Osmond performers had been on, even if only briefly.

Marie vaguely recalls sharing a short song and dance with Andy when she was only four or five, but it was too informal to be considered her real professional debut.

The show's cancellation did not end their good working relationship with Andy; he was still in demand on the club circuit, and the Osmonds were happy to go along. Without Andy's firm backing at this juncture in their career, they easily could have faded from show business. But he believed in them so strongly that the Osmonds were the first act he signed to record for his brand new record label, Barnaby Records. The four LPs they had recorded for MGM never made a ripple in the industry, and that label was in trouble, so Andy was giving them a nice break.

Family groups were the rage of the late '60s. The ones getting the most attention, though, were the Cowsills and The Five Stairsteps and Cubie. Meanwhile the Osmonds were singing Dixieland and doing softshoe routines to "Fascinatin' Rhythm" behind Andy. The first two singles they released for Andy's company, "Mary Elizabeth" and "Speak Like A Child," received fair reviews and some airplay, but they seemed to lack a sound that appealed to the major portion of record buyers—their fellow teenagers. Despite their lack of sales, they had plenty of work.

And, of course, they were not allowed to neglect their education. While doing Andy's series, they had to be tutored three hours a day, by virtue of California's strict child labor laws. Nor did Olive let them forget their chores. They may have been earning thousands of dollars a week, but they still did dishes, swept, and took out the garbage. Everything was shared equally as the Osmonds did not believe in hiring help when there were so many strong hands in the house. When they went on tour, the kids took along correspondence courses and Olive supervised their homework, as always. The trips also were an educational experience as Olive read up on all the cities and countries they visited and made sure they saw whatever historical sights were available.

At this point, Marie was satisfied to sit on the sidelines and emulate her mother. Content with learning how to cook and sew, Marie was Olive's little shadow. As a child, Marie was a bit chubby and did not look like a likely candidate for the family's act. Olive was just as pleased to have a chatty, constant companion. On tour, while the boys rehearsed, Olive and Marie would busy themselves in local shops. Olive passed her passion for fashion designing along to her only daughter. Some of their happiest moments were spent shopping for patterns and fabrics. Marie was allowed free rein in expressing her own fashion flair; Olive would let her browse through the big pattern books and choose her own styles. Once the pattern was bought, they would spend more hours fingering fabrics, discussing the merits of each until Marie found what she wanted. Marie saved the scraps to make doll clothes, which was a good way to practice before making the real thing.

With such pastimes, it was obvious that the Osmonds were never caught up in the glittery phoniness of show business. They were bound by their traditions, not the least of which was that Mormon girls are raised with one important purpose in life—to be good wives and to bear children to perpetuate the family. There were times when Olive heard Marie singing that she sensed real talent, but, unlike with the boys, Marie's talents were not encouraged to any great extent. For her, singing might be a pleasant hobby, but her number one priority should be to marry.

To that end, when Marie was seven, Olive told her that she was old enough to start her hope chest. That might sound hopelessly outdated to most people, a custom that has gone the way of the bustle for the rest of the country. But the little girl was ecstatic. She still remembers their first purchase for the precious box: a beautiful, handmade blanket they found in a little shop in Sweden. From then on, Marie bought linens and silverware and all sorts of fine items in shops around the world. Along the way she developed a love of shopping, and Donny has always kidded that if Marie could only do one thing in the world for the rest of her life, it would be shopping!

The trip to Sweden marked another first for Marie. Her brothers introduced her from the stage and she joined them for a song. Despite this exposure, the dark-haired, brown-eyed tot harbored no secret desires to get into the act. Little Jimmy, on the other hand, was chomping at the bit to be part of the fun.

The family continued to work steadily, especially in Las Vegas, where their clean-cut song and dance routines were a favorite. Unlike television or the movies, Vegas audiences did not care whether an act had a hit record or not, as long as they made everyone feel good after the show. That is what the Osmonds did best. Often, though they were only an opening act and not the stars, the Osmonds brought home the good reviews. Oddly, during this period, when they were not making the charts, they received some of their best notices.

In 1969, Donny celebrated his twelfth birthday with his family in Las Vegas, where they were appearing with a Marty Allen revue at Caesars Palace. According to *Variety*, the show business bible, the Osmonds' half-hour opening segment was "whammo." The reviewer continued by saying that Marty Allen was clearly in trouble the rest of the night because the Osmonds were "a rough act to follow or insert within an existing framework, with the result that Osmond bows and cheers are a stopper and Allen has to rev up his revue on Mt. Everest." What impressed the reviewer the most was the Osmonds' versatility. "They blow instrumentally, whirl out on terpery and slice up the music with engaging comedy." Here Donny was singled out for the comedy style he would one day employ in his and Marie's TV series. "Donny, 11, is the foil in many of the antics," the writer said, "dishing out 'awful' jokes as a running gag." And it all led to a socko finish with none other than Jimmy, who had recently become a regular in the act. The review stated that the six-year-old had brought down the house, rocking on "I Got A Woman."

Reviews such as that made the Osmonds favorites with the Las Vegas Strip hotel crowd. They had all the bookings they could handle, and it was in Vegas that they really honed their musical skills. On television and with Andy they had been mainly back-up singers, but in Vegas they could give free range to their diverse talents. The brothers were proficient on several instruments, but eventually Alan took over lead guitar, Wayne guitar and saxophone, Merrill the bass, Jay the drums, and Donny became the keyboard man.

There were other advantages to their Vegas stints. It was close to Utah and the farm they appreciated more than ever. Between engagements, they actually found themselves enjoying baling hay and cleaning stables and all the other chores. Of course, it helped that they knew farm work was only temporary! And rarely did a day go by without some kind of baseball or football game.

Being home for a spell also meant that Alan, Merrill, and Wayne had the quiet time necessary to write new songs. A decade in the music business had taught them that musical acts are judged by their success on the pop charts, not by constant employment. If they were to become really popular they would have to find the right sound or style to make the charts.

Most of the lead vocals had been handled by Alan and Wayne, but there was no denying young Donny's impact on the teenyboppers who had caught their act in Vegas. With his big, bright, doe-soft eyes, ringed by incredibly long, dark eyelashes, Donny was the handsomest brother in the family. And he was also a natural singer with a good sense of rhythm. Alan, Wayne, and Merrill wrote tight harmonies for the brothers and Donny had no trouble keeping up his end.

With another recording date coming up, the brothers decided it was time to let Donny sing lead on a few of the cuts. They tried to spread everything around evenly, and he was just the right age for one of the songs they planned to put on the album.

Wayne and Alan were the ones who closely supervised recording dates. Alan was an electronics expert, and both understood how to manipulate multi-tracks to mix and match the orchestra and voices. Recording has become more of an electronic science than a matter of voice. But what they wanted to do on Donny's lead—a bright and bouncy number, titled "One Bad Apple" that was obviously aimed at young girls—was to really "punch up" his voice.

What happened next, after the song was sent out to disc jockeys, caught even the professional Osmonds completely by surprise. That single became the building block for the Osmond empire, an empire that would make them one of the wealthiest families in the entertainment industry!

3

Osmondmania

In one twelve-month period between 1971 and 1972, eleven Osmond records went gold, which was better than even Elvis and the Beatles had done at the height of their popularity. It all started with the recording of "One Bad Apple," which was released as a single from the Osmonds' LP, *Osmonds*. The single hit the charts with a bullet, signifying immediate popularity with record buyers. But while it was off of an Osmond album, there was no denying that the real power behind its success was Donny.

The record world is a volatile business. Changes happen rapidly and without warning. By 1971, the older buyers who favored such stars as Perry Como and Patti Page had been put on a back burner as the youth wave hit the market. Even the younger group was split in half between the 13-to-25 crowd who wanted hard, driving rock from Three Dog Night, Rod Stewart, or Janis Joplin, and the 8- to 13-year-olds who identified with less sexually explosive stars. The kiddie power crowd literally fell at sweet-faced Donny Osmond's feet after he completed "One Bad Apple." It was a song each girl believed was directed right at her, a song about a boy pining for a girl who had been hurt by a previous "bad apple." It was innocent; it was bland; and so was the small, slender, boy delivering the lyric. He was a nice, safe, preteen that girls could fantasize about, and parents were enchanted with.

Suddenly, Donny's face was peering out from magazine racks around the world as he became a kind of cottage industry for magazine publishers. "What Kind Of Girl Is Donny Looking For?" and "What Is Donny Osmond Really Like?" were sure-fire questions to get girls to spend their allowances for a chance to read the answers.

And that is when the Osmonds surprised many people, even within the show business community, with their rigid life style. Teen magazines loved to run "Win a Date" contests with whatever preteen was then driving little girls wild. But that was impossible with Donny because, as he cheerfully explained, Osmonds were not allowed to date until they were 16! And then they had to double with a relative until they were 18! It sounded like something out of the middle ages—or the 1950s, and what made it odder was that Donny approved. Nothing, however, hurt him with the young girls who bought his records and any other Donny items they could get their hands on.

Just weeks after its release, "One Bad Apple" hit the number one spot on all the music charts, and there it remained for a phenomenal five weeks. It was the first Osmond record ever even to make the charts, which are usually reserved for the 150 best-selling singles and albums in any given week.

The brothers, and their record company, were quick to jump on the bandwagon with followup records. In 1971 alone, the Osmonds had two solid-selling LPs: *Osmonds*, which hit the top 15 and was on the list for 43 weeks, and *Homemade*, which lasted 34 weeks in the top 100. Besides "One Bad Apple," another single off an album, "Yo Yo," went all the way to number three. The Osmond Brothers had become firmly established.

Donny, however, was the real phenomenon! That same year, he brought out two hot sellers, *The Donny Osmond Album*, which contained his number one single, "Go Away Little Girl" (three weeks on top), and *To You With Love*. From those two LPs, aside from "Little Girl," he also rocketed up the charts with "Hey Girl," "Sweet and Innocent," and "I Knew You When."

Success like that was sweet, but not without its drawbacks. Donny could not walk down the street without being followed by hordes of junior high school girls. He was glad most of his fans were well dressed and well behaved, but it was still a nuisance. He, of course, could not let on if he was annoyed and always behaved in the manner he had been raised.

The most amazing aspect of teen idolism is that it is practically a license to print money. The hit records are just the beginning. The real profit is from the spinoffs—the personal appearances for which red-hot acts can make upwards of $50,000 per night, posters, buttons, and all kinds of merchandising tie-ins. Donny overnight became the Osmonds' gold mine.

When this kind of superstardom happens, people in the industry hold their breath to see how long it takes the new sensation to freak out on a star trip. It happens to nearly every star, teen or adult, and usually involves an entourage of hangers-on who dote on the star's every word—as long as he keeps picking up the tabs. These groups inevitably dissolve about the same time the star disappears from the charts, only to resurface again when the next new sensation comes along. At the height of this period, the said star can do no wrong and nobody seems to do anything right enough for the "chosen one." Often the money is siphoned off into the accounts of agents, managers, and friends who have been silent business partners. This was not going to be the story of Donny Osmond.

Outwardly, there was no perceptible change in the Osmonds' life style even though they were coining millions. They certainly did not live lavishly, although they lived comfortably in the apartment house they had bought in Los Angeles. There were three upstairs and four downstairs apartments, so that the older boys could have their privacy. They turned the basement into a recording studio, where the brothers liked to fool around with new sounds. Now that they were on top, they were determined to stay there.

George controlled their investments, just as he always did, but he now included Alan in many of the decisions, since he seemed the likely heir to the business side of the family. Olive was interested in the mail order business they began and expanded when Donny turned into a teen idol. "I used to love mail order offers," Olive has said. "I used penny postcards to send for free Tangee lipsticks, Lady Esther powder, and free recipes." Now, she decided, was the time to put her knowledge to good use as teenagers had not changed much; they still loved to send for precious merchandise unavailable through other sources. The Osmond fan club, which had been around for some time, quadrupled in size because of Donny.

Best of all, their new popularity opened the door for Virl and Tom to be a part of the family entertainment enterprise. They took the photos of the brothers that were sold through the mail and supervised all the printing of catalogues and posters. Now, it truly was a family business and the more help Tom and Virl could give, the less bitter they felt about the old days, when no one seemed to have time for them. There was a new camaraderie in the Osmond household. Olive believed the family was truly blessed. Even Jimmy got in the business when Olive gave him a button machine for Christmas, and he turned out many of the tens of thousands that were sold at Osmond concerts. Demand was so great, Jimmy had to hire a friend to keep up the supply. Olive recognized a fine opportunity to give her youngest child a thorough grounding in finance, and thus expected him to take care of his own purchases for his enterprise and to keep track of his profits. Jimmy felt very important when Olive let him borrow a secretary and bookkeeper from the family's office to help with his button business. When Jimmy joined the act, of course, he had to give up his button activity, but the expertise he picked up from being responsible for it is still there.

Donny's popularity kept the family on the move. An extensive concert tour was planned with Donny as the centerpiece. It was an exciting time for all of them, and with so many details to be worked out, nobody thought twice when Donny mentioned one day that he was not feeling well.

Normally, they are a concerned family whenever one member is ailing. But Donny's complaint of a stomach ache was a familiar one. The mysterious ache had troubled him for nearly five years. Doctors were consulted, but no one could explain why he suffered. Usually Donny would lie down, and in a day or two, the ache would clear up and he would be fine.

This time, however, Donny's stomach was worse than ever. Doubled up in pain, he lay on his bed while the family sought help. When they arrived with him at the hospital, the doctors took one look and knew they would have to operate. For all those years, Donny had been suffering from a bad appendix, and if the family had not acted quickly this time, Donny would have died.

"Donny O" lovers around the world were relieved to hear that he would be fine and soon up and around on his tour. There was no way he would disappoint his fans. Presents poured into the hospital, most of which the Osmonds donated to worthy organizations.

Between tours, now more than ever, the Osmonds looked forward to their vacations in Ogden. There they could relax and rest up, away from the crowds that were like shadows, following wherever their idol went.

But even their trips back home were more complicated than before. In the days when they were doing the *Andy Williams Show*, they had just traveled by station wagon, with Donny and Jimmy claiming the back of the wagon as a playground where they could pitch a tent of blankets and pretend to camp out. Donny told ghost stories to his little brother that kept the boy up all night. The trips had been leisurely and fun.

Once their fame increased, so did their entourage. Instead of one simple wagon, they now needed a regular caravan, with a truck for their equipment, a camper, and a station wagon. Of course, the older boys now had driver's licenses, which made this mode of travel easier, but it was also a sign of their success.

Being home-lovers, the Osmonds always tried to be in Utah for the important holidays like Christmas and Thanksgiving. It was a time to gather the families together, to visit with Virl and Tom, who were married and had children of their own. Virl's wife, Chris, and Tom's spouse, Lyn, were very dear to Olive, and in the few weeks they could all be together, she tried to spend time with each family member individually to learn what she had missed between visits. It made for a lively household.

As in most large families, the Osmonds had established their own gift-giving setup. There were just too many for everyone to exchange with everyone else, so they drew names from a stocking, which made it even more mysterious. No one knew who was giving them a gift!

In 1971, Donny was one of the names Marie pulled out of the stocking, and after a great deal of thought, she knew just what she wanted to give America's top teen idol! It was meant to be a gag gift, but when Donny dashed downstairs on Christmas morning to find that his sister had stuffed thirty pairs of purple socks in his stocking, he was delighted. There was not one teenybopper in America who did not know that purple was Donny's absolutely "fave" color, and now he decided he had enough pairs so that he wouldn't have to wear any other type of socks again. From then on, Donny's purple socks became his trademark. For years to come, his family had to buy white socks and dye them, as purple socks are hard to come by in stores.

The Osmonds had another treat in store that year; they were voted the most popular singing act in the world, thanks to Donny and "One Bad Apple." Not only American teens, but Japanese, Australian, and English kids idolized the handsome 14-year-old with the winning smile and ingratiating manners.

The Osmonds rang in 1972 by rushing into production with more records. In that super-successful year, Donny's *Portrait of Donny* would race up to the number-six spot on the top album list and remain in the Top 100 for thirty-six weeks. His other two LPs that year, *Too Young* and *My Best To You*, were also highly successful. There were four best-selling singles from them, too—"Puppy Love," "Why," "Too Young," and "Lonely Boy."

The Osmond Brothers (with Donny, natch) also put three long-players in the top 100—*Phase III, The Osmonds*

"*Live*," and *Crazy Horses*—along with two single cuts from the albums—"Crazy Horses" and "Hold Her Tight." As a change of pace, the brothers also collaborated with a couple of other MGM recording stars, Steve Lawrence and Eydie Gorme, who had had their share of hits, too, for a joint single titled "We Can Make It Together."

Even little Jimmy got on the hit wagon with his *Killer Joe* album. His single, "Long-Haired Lover From Liverpool," reached 105 on the American charts, but it was more important for establishing him as a superstar in England, and especially in Japan, where he was even bigger than Donny!

Aside from Virl and Tom, the only Osmond hanging back was Marie, but she was beginning to exhibit signs of talent and interest. Her public appearances had been few and far between, really consisting of her stage bow in Sweden and a 1970 duet she had done with Donny on "Raindrops Keep Falling On My Head" on their foreign tour. When she sang on Family Night, Olive noted that Marie had a sweet country/western style and encouraged her in that direction.

One reason Marie may have been prompted to get involved was because she was discovering boys. But, like all teenage girls, she was worried about her looks. Marie admits that she had a terrible inferiority complex as a young girl. She had a weight problem, much worse in her head, of course, than in real life, so she put herself on a diet. It wasn't easy because Marie loves ice cream, but it didn't love her, except around the hips! Between the ages of eleven and thirteen, Marie slimmed down some thirty-five pounds, which helped her gain self-confidence. Still, Marie was three years away from dating. The family's policy of no dates until sixteen was very strict, one of the hard-and-fast rules. Of all the Osmonds, Marie, probably because she was the only girl, and girls mature faster than boys, was the most anxious to reach that magical age when she could go out.

Donny liked girls and had done his share of innocent flirting, but he saw so many teenyboppers at his concerts that he seemed almost relieved to be denied dating privileges. Donny's idea of relaxing was to sit down with an inspirational book for self-improvement or with one of his electronics magazines to read about his favorite hobby. He is a whiz at electronics and, along with Alan, has always installed most of the equipment in their various recording studios. The other Osmonds knew better than to try to get Donny's attention when he was absorbed in one of his projects.

In a way, it was lucky that Donny had hobbies he could enjoy alone or with one of his brothers, because he was paying a price for his idoldom. Marie is not afraid to admit that there were times growing up with her talented family when she longed for a more normal life, to go to a regular school instead of getting tutored, to go to friends' homes instead of always being on her own on the road. But, looking back from an adult perspective, she realizes that she was one of the rare lucky people who has traveled the world instead of being stuck in one small town, and she has shopped in every major city on the map. Now she would not trade places with anyone.

Donny, too, faced difficulties when he was a teenager. For him, the trouble was not on the road, but back in Ogden. In any town, there is always a small percentage of jealous people who envy anyone with talent and ambition. To Donny's dismay, Ogden, even with its large Mormon population, was not immune to the tendency. His leap to superstardom made him a visible target whenever he went into town. Naturally, it is not easy for those who have grown up with you to suddenly be reading about you in the papers or to find your face smiling down from magazine racks in shops and supermarkets all over town. He cannot hide the pain in his voice whenever he talks about those days in Ogden; the psychological scars are obviously still apparent. He has vivid memories of being attacked. "Thugs threw dirt clods and apple cores at me," he has said. "That hurts both emotionally and literally." Nor did he make many friends back then as "all throughout my teenage years," he says, "I was never accepted because I was a teenybopper in the magazines." Fortunately, he had his brothers and Marie for best friends.

Outside of Ogden, it would have been hard to form close

friendships, too, not only because of the constant traveling, but because his values were so different from other teenagers. Smoking, drinking, drugs, stimulants, sex—all were taboo for his family. Most California teens lived life in the fast lane through the '70s, putting them at odds with the Osmonds' strict moral standards.

Probably none of this would have mattered much if Donny's superstardom had not brought a prying press into the Osmond's private lives. It would be hard to sort out which came first, the "goody-goody" image from their interviews, or the sometimes cruel record reviews from writers who saved their raves for the drugged-out rockers while tossing the Osmonds off as pure pap. Writing about one of their albums for *Life* magazine in 1972, Albert Goldman, the noted rock music critic, dismissed the group's efforts, declaring somewhat snidely that "the Osmonds are the little white knights of soul." Other major reviewers for such heavyweight music magazines as *Creem, Audio,* and *Circus* usually rated their releases from fair to poor.

But then, teen idols usually take such reviews in stride. Their music is not meant to please serious buffs, but little girls who buy up everything in sight on and about their stars. Donny genuinely liked his audiences and was not about to alter his music or his life style to fit the current fashion. Their music had not made much of a ripple in the 1960s, but once Donny dared to appeal to the teenybopper set, it was interesting how savage some reviewers could be, almost as if they were jealous of his success. At this time the Osmonds made no pretense of attempting to compete with Nilsson or Al Green or Neil Young, or even with the Jackson Five, the new black family making the charts.

In later years, the Osmonds would be compared, not always favorably, with the black group, and less knowledgeable writers would hint that the Osmonds had copied the Jacksons, not realizing that the Osmonds had been around the music scene many years before them. In fact, some say the Jacksons had admired the Osmonds on the *Andy Williams Show* and patterned themselves after the Utah five!

The reviews, good or bad, had little impact on the Osmonds; whatever they recorded sold in the millions. Between 1971 and 1976, they sold over 70 million records worldwide and have twenty-one gold records to show for it.

Early in 1973, Marie realized that everyone in the family was toiling away in show business but her. Virl and Tom cranked out most of the posters and publicity material from Utah, with Olive writing the monthly newsletter for Donny's adoring fans as well as being the driving force behind the thriving mail-order business. This was worth all the years of living out of suitcases and prodding her brood on to succeed. While it is true that the brothers all had a natural flair and love of entertaining, those who have worked with the Osmonds over the years have one common thought: Olive Osmond is the force behind the throne, the one who had the vision and who inspired the boys to drive themselves a little harder each year; she was the one who never quit, and it was her determination that kept the group together until they reached the top. Though she stays demurely in the background, press agents, photographers and writers always say, "Mrs. Osmond is the one to watch. She works very quietly behind the scenes, but she is the guiding hand they all depend upon, make no mistake!" Papa George, of course, was the stated head of the enterprise, the one who handled the investments, though again, insiders add that it was Olive who spent most of the time in the office, overseeing the family's entire operation. And all the boys, including Jimmy naturally, rehearsed, recorded, and threw themselves into performing. Only Marie seemed to have no specific duties in the organization.

That spring, the brothers went back to Las Vegas, explaining to writers who questioned their stints in such a den of iniquity, that their moral principles were a private matter and restricted to their family and other devout Mormons, and that they were not public moralizers. While they could not in good conscience condone the gambling, drinking, legal prostitution, and the like that drew millions of eager visitors yearly, neither did they feel obliged to condemn it. "Live and let live" was their motto, and as long as the people left their show smiling and feeling good, they had done their part. Others may see a conflict between their beliefs and entertaining in Vegas, but the Osmonds had clear consciences.

Meanwhile, there were plans afoot to get Marie on stage. Newly slim, she was glad to join Donny on stage at Caesars Palace for a duet on "Where Is The Love," and she must have enjoyed the applause because not long after, her brothers had her in the recording studio. Alan, Wayne, and Merrill, who were the ones most involved in the family recordings, agreed with Olive's early estimation of Marie's voice, and the thirteen-year-old put together an album around an old country pop tune, "Paper Roses."

In no time at all, it seemed, it was the Donny-phenomenon all over again. The single shot into the Top 10 with amazing speed, as did the LP. Best of all, the family act was complete with each child responsible for himself or herself while working for the good of the whole. It was working out exactly as Olive and George had dreamed.

Donny was not idle either in 1973, hitting the charts with his cuts of "Twelfth of Never," "A Million to One," and "Young Love." Alan, Wayne, Merrill, Jay, and Donny were successful on "Let Me In" and "Goin' Home." Rarely a day went by without an Osmond song dominating the airwaves.

Nor was their success confined to America. When Donny and company arrived in England, his fans went wild! They called it "Osmondmania," and with good reason. Ten thousand fans turned up to watch the Osmonds land at Heathrow Airport just outside London that October. They were arriving for a series of concerts, but the British teenyboppers could not wait to get a glimpse of their young idol. As the plane landed, a roof garden packed with fans had a fence give way, and scores of girls fell off the balcony. The London police had never seen anything to match the frenzy awaiting the Osmonds arrival, and the next day, a debate raged throughout the country whether to ban pop groups from that major airport thereafter.

The Osmondmania was so hysterical, Donny had to be sneaked into and out of the hotel. Drummer Buddy Rich was lucky to get out of town alive after he went on Michael

Parkinson's popular talk show in London (the equivalent of the *Tonight* show in America), and exclaimed that the Osmonds "have no talent" and that he was "mystified by young people's adoration of them."

Their concerts were sellouts, and magazines sprang up around the country devoted to Donny's doings—as well as those of the rest of the family. In England, each of the brothers had his own following, even Jay, who was always the quietest of the bunch. Long after the original quartet had faded into the background in America, leaving center stage to Donny and Marie, Alan, Merrill, Jay, and Wayne remained pinup attractions in England.

The older Osmonds sensed that their era was ending back home, at least when it came to performing. There was no resentment, just a shrewd reading of the market. And Alan and Wayne were prepared to shift gears when necessary to meet whatever the market demanded. If at the time that meant Donny, Marie, and Jimmy, that's what they would give the public. No ego clashes were involved because the Osmonds were still operating as one unit. Donny and Marie were the properties on showcase, but behind the scenes, their brothers guided their choice of music, the arrangements, and, in fact, supervised every aspect of their acts. And they all shared equally in the profits.

Meanwhile, the older brothers had more on their minds than singing. Whenever their schedules permitted, Olive made sure they returned to Utah, only instead of going to their Ogden farm the family would stay at yet another of their properties, a large complex apartment that was situated across the street from Brigham Young University in Provo. Olive had an eye on the future when the family made this purchase. Not only was it a good financial investment, since it provided simple, clean housing for the university students who lived off campus, but it paved the way for her children to meet the best and brightest Mormons in the world. BYU is run by the Mormons, and the faithful from the world over come to the school, not only because it provides an excellent education, but because, as Olive knew, it was a good place to meet marriage partners.

Some might say that Olive ran her large family like a

professional chess player, moving her children around, manipulating them to her advantage, and finally mating each in turn as coolly and unemotionally as a grandmaster. If so, none of them has ever complained, at least publicly, and all of the children, so far, have been happy with their mates.

Merrill was the first of the singing brothers to wed. Friends had introduced him to a pretty, young schoolteacher. He did not need much time to make up his mind that he wanted to marry Mary Carlson, although his family thought he was too young. Merrill listened as politely as ever to his mother and father, but he explained that though he was only twenty, he knew that Mary was the one he wanted to be by his side. Since he was so sure, his parents gave their blessing and in September 17, 1973, Merrill and Mary and their immediate families met inside the great Mormon Temple in Salt Lake City and exchanged the vows that would bind them not only in this life but for all eternity, in accordance with the church's beliefs.

The newlyweds did not have much time to themselves before Merrill had to join the family on that English tour that turned into a wild frenzy, but they continued the honeymoon in England, and Mary had a wonderful time.

Merrill and Mary seemed the perfect advertisement for marital bliss, and soon Alan and Wayne followed their footsteps. Alan apparently spotted his bride-to-be, Suzanne Pinegar, at a BYU basketball game. The Osmonds frequently mingled with the students in Provo and audited as many classes as they could squeeze in. Despite his fame and wealth, Suzanne showed little interest when Alan introduced himself to her.

Like the Osmonds, Suzanne had been brought up to obey strict rules, one of which was not to spend time with men to whom she had not been properly introduced—that meant by family or close friends. Fortunately, when Alan mentioned the pretty cheerleader to his brother Merrill and Mary the following day, Mary knew Suzanne and called to arrange a proper date for the twosome. Under those circumstances, Suzanne could not help but find the handsome six-foot singer charming. And it was obvious that he was smitten with the girl with green eyes and golden hair.

Olive readily approved of Alan's choice, especially since Suzanne's father was an educator. The Osmonds once again trooped into the Mormon Temple on July 16, 1974, to see Alan and Suzanne united for eternity.

Naturally, anytime an Osmond dated, he had to warn the girl what was ahead for her if she married into the family. Half the year they lived like gypsies, often traveling in a big bus from concert to concert, eating, sleeping, and trying to get along in cramped quarters—so the girls had to be flexible and compatible. Suzanne understood what she might have to do to be a good wife, so she was not surprised, a few days after the ceremony, to find herself in Las Vegas where her husband had a singing engagement with his brothers.

When they weren't on stage, the brothers would rehearse their new single as it was to be introduced to the world on the prestigious *Tonight* show two weeks later in Hollywood. The late-night talk show is the industry's premiere showcase for new material, and only the top acts are invited to bring in new songs, which in that one performance can be heard by millions of viewers. Captive audiences like that are hard to come by, so the Osmonds were honored to be invited on the show. They hoped the new song would broaden their market, as they were trying to capture one of the new pop sounds on the upswing with a soul-flavored effort—something the kids could dance to in large numbers. Wayne thought they had succeeded with "Love Me For A Reason," which he called "good boogie music."

True to the show's tradition, after they sang it for the *Tonight* audience, the Osmond tune hit the national charts, making the Top 10, the last single recorded by all the brothers that would do so well. But there was more news from the group. Not only were they broadening their record market, but their show business careers were taking a turn toward movies. They were taking some time away from music to develop film scripts, one of which they hoped to star in by the following year. Unfortunately nothing came of their movie ideas, although they were sure such a move was inevitable.

In the meantime, Wayne was falling in love. Friends had

introduced him to one of the most beautiful girls in the world. Her name was Kathlyn White, and the proof of her beauty was the fact that she had been crowned Miss Utah. If she had been only an ambitious girl, that might have been a stumbling block in her relationship with Wayne. Ahead of her was the Miss America contest with its $100,000 prize, and modeling and acting opportunities. That was a package most women would have found too attractive to turn down. But Kathy had no qualms about going to the contest organizers and asking to be relieved of her crown. When she did that, all of the Osmonds knew that Wayne had found a special and wonderful girl. Kathlyn became Mrs. Melvin Wayne Osmond on December 13, 1974.

Of all the Osmonds, Marie was probably the happiest when her brothers got married; she found herself with three new sisters and she has remained close to all of them. Besides, it meant she could have her pick of the available bedrooms in her parents' homes. As each brother married, he was given a lovely new home, which is each Osmonds' due at the right time. It was all part of the joint-sharing plan George and Olive had devised for the children's money. When they reached driving age, each child was given a new car; upon marrying, he or she received the house and an increase in their monthly allowance from the family fund. As children were born, the monthly draw was also increased. Otherwise, all the money was in the common investment fund. Despite the fact that Donny, and later Marie, brought in ten to twenty times as much money as any of the others, neither has ever resented this plan, and it has worked for the good of all.

And Alan's dream was coming true: the brothers were living side by side. Not even marriages could come between their tight-knit relationship. Now Alan's plans were becoming even more grandiose; he envisioned an entire city of Osmonds and spoke often of the idea with his father. George thought it was a splendid idea, as he was as worried about bad influences reaching his grandchildren as he had once been about the boys and Marie. While Alan had the dream, only George had the power to put it to work, so he set about looking for a good piece of real estate.

In the meantime, Jay was dating several pretty co-eds but was in no rush to be like his brothers and marry. He often took Donny along on double dates, but so far, he had not experienced a bout of "Puppy Love." And Marie was just one year—one long year in her mind—away from dating boys.

The main course of business, however, remained their careers. Donny's popularity was holding up, although his record sales were diminishing. Perhaps it was time for yet another quick change of pace. *Paper Roses'* success, both as a single and an album, and her subsequent *My Little Corner of the World*, moved Marie into the superstar stratosphere. The records were popular on both important fronts—with the fans, who sent them to gold, as well as with the critics. Marie's mellow country style made her the first Osmond to get high marks from the music press. In fact, when the Grammy nominations were in, Marie was thrilled to be among the nominees, the first Osmond ever to be so-honored. There was no denying her importance to the act now.

Donny's fans were including Marie in their affection. Not that anyone could be as sensational as their fantasy figure, but little girls took note of Marie's figure and the clothes she wore. Teaming the brother and sister up seemed the most natural move to the ever-shrewd, show-biz wise Osmonds.

Donny and Marie liked the idea. They had always been close in the same way as Alan and Wayne, and Merrill and Jay, had paired off. That happens in big families; it is easiest to form friendship with the sibling closest to your own age. And with their four older brothers working on their singing most of the time, Donny and Marie had been playmates.

Their easy banter and casual acceptance of each other reflected that special bond they shared. It was also reflected in their first LP together, *I'm Leaving It All Up To You*. The blend of their voices was appealing, and disc jockeys were deluged with requests for their duet. The title single and the album added two more gold records to the family's Utah walls.

It was a pleasant surprise to the Osmonds to discover how the fans responded to the cute pair of teenagers. Neither lost their fans, both gained from the arrangement. Over the next four years, Donny and Marie turned out a steady stream of top tunes. with "Morning Side of the Mountain," "Make The World Go Away," and "Deep Purple," the most popular.

When the family brought their show to Las Vegas, the Donny and Marie spots were the highlights. The Osmond Family generally spent six to eight weeks a year in Las Vegas, usually at the Tropicana, where they brought in a nice family crowd.

Vegas bosses usually prefered Frank Sinatra or Johnny Carson because they were sure-fire draws with the high rollers and the big-money gamblers, but the Osmonds were responsible for introducing many of their nice middle-class fans to the town. And Sinatra, Carson, and the few other big money acts could not play Vegas fifty-two weeks a year; the Osmonds were an agreeable compromise, and their slick act went over well.

Although the Osmonds had hit the jackpot in records, concerts, and night clubs, and were the most popular teen act in the world, they were still not satisfied. Their drive and ambition turned their talents toward television and movies, the two biggest prizes in show business.

The major stumbling block to any television appearance was the fact that the Osmonds commanded a very young audience; no one considered them as appealing to the essential prime time target audience, the sophisticated eighteen-to thirty-nine-year-olds. Therefore, the chances of ever being offered their own series were remote. Osmonds were wonderful guest stars and guaranteed the teenybopper set, but it was feared that their too-good-to-be-true image would produce a dull show and might turn off the older viewers for the rest of the evening. Television depends on one strong show leading into the next so that networks can win an entire evening's ratings. One point differences can mean the addition or loss of millions of dollars. It was feared that the Osmonds would not be a strong lead-in to the rest of an evening's lineup, and they would have to be given the first spot, eight to nine o'clock, before their fans were put to bed. All in all, television and the Osmonds seemed worlds apart.

Still, their friendly personalities and recording popularity had to be recognized. And television is a voracious medium, eating up more performers than any other form of entertainment. Every year TV raises one or two entertainers to superstardom, where they are lauded, fawned over, and treated like royalty. And every year, several of those who have enjoyed that rarified atmosphere are deposited on the scrap heap, never to be seen again. To be sure, they retire very wealthy if they have hired good managers, but that is poor compensation for the shattered ego of a performer that can no longer attract crowds or adoring sycophants.

There is no sadder sight than watching yesterday's star wandering alone down Sunset Boulevard, a has-been, yesterday's news. But that is the tragic ending for many onetime television stars. The medium sucks them up and then it spits them out. This creates an endless demand for new stars, new material, new ideas. And the Osmonds seemed like naturals for at least a chance. Still, there was their image. Somehow they would just have to find a way of proving their popularity.

Even as young as twelve and ten, Donny and Marie had those great big grins (*photo: Frank Edwards Fotos International*).

At Caesars Palace with their nightclub act in 1970, the kids left the pool long enough for this photo session (*photo: Frank Edwards Fotos International*).

Teen idols Donny and Marie were real trendsetters at the height of their TV show's popularity (*photo: London Daily Express*).

The Osmonds are very sports-loving, and Marie looked to big brother Donny to give her a few batting tips from time to time. There was always some kind of game going when they were home on their farm in Utah (*photo: Transworld Feature Syndicate, inc.*).

Mary Carlson learns what it means to marry an Osmond as her groom Merrill and his brothers hustle her away from fans on their wedding day (*photo: Nicholas Allen*).

A rare occasion—Olive and George with no little Osmonds lurking nearby (*photo: Frank Edwards Fotos International*).

Mealtimes are special to the Osmonds; it gives them a chance to catch up on what each has been doing. Clockwise from left: Marie, Merrill, Wayne, Alan, Jay, Donny, Olive, Jimmy, and George (*photo: London Daily Express*).

Despite the sibling rivalry image they promoted for their series, Marie and Donny were really very close. They often attended industry events together (*photo: Frank Edwards Fotos International*).

The closeknit clan believes the family that plays together stays together, which is why everyone goes along on concert tours. Here from left to right is Merrill and Mary, Alan and Suzanne, Wayne, George, Jimmy, Olive, Jay, Marie, and Donny, who were visiting a stately English mansion between London concerts (*photo: London Daily Express*).

Osmondmania gripped London's teenage girls when their favorite group hit town. The family was concerned about the shrieking fans—and their own safety (*photo: London Daily Express*).

It's the McOsmonds as the youngsters show off some souvenir tam o'shanters they had picked up abroad. Everyone in the family is an inveterate collector. Back row left to right: Alan, Merrill, Wayne. Seated left to right: Donny, Marie, Jimmy, and Jay (*photo: London Daily Express*).

Donny and Marie said "aloha" to their Hawaiian fans when they arrived in Honolulu to film their first, and so far last, feature film, *Goin' Coconuts* (*photo: Lee Sporkin*).

When Donny and Marie's variety hour debuted on ABC-TV, they were the youngest entertainers ever to host their very own series (*photo: Pictorial Parade*).

The popular singing duo were honored with the People's Choice award in 1979. Brooke Shields presented the statue to them (*photo: Frank Edwards Fotos International*).

Marie was game to try anything on her TV series, but she was such a perfectionist, these rigorous routines often left her exhausted (*photo: Bob Grant Fotos International*).

All grown up, the talented family made their London farewell appearances in 1980. It was the end of an era (*photo: London Daily Express*).

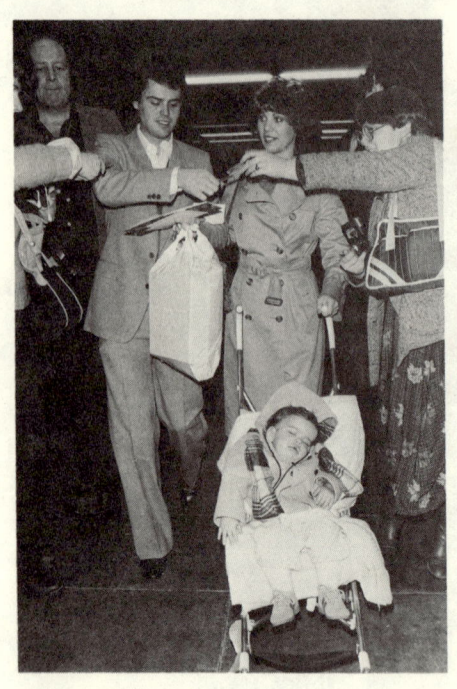

Donny tries to take Debbie and their sons on all of his tours. Donny, Jr., (just eight months old here) obviously is not impressed with his dad's stardom (*photo: London Daily Express*).

Donny, sporting his new beard, hosting the New Year's Eve festivities in the Waldorf-Astoria's Grand Ballroom on December 31, 1982 (*photo: taken by Star Black, courtesy of Waldorf-Astoria*).

Steve Craig and Marie pose prettily shortly after their 1982 wedding (*photo: Ira Berger*).

4

A Little Bit Country, A Little Bit Rock 'n' Roll

Wherever they roamed, the Osmonds wore their patriotism, faith, and virtuousness like a badge of honor. It was all part of their mission to stand up in the middle of a society that was accommodating drugs, sexual liberties, and liberated women, living proof that young people still had a choice, that there was another way open to them that could bring them greater personal happiness. Unfortunately, when their quotes appeared selectively in interviews, it made them sound antiseptic to the point of being boring. Principles and strong moral convictions were hard things to sell.

While other teenagers and kids out of college were struggling to be free of what they considered parental demands and rules, there were the Osmond children chirping that "Every decision made concerning our careers is a family decision. And once a week, the family also has a meeting to discuss personal goals and the things we hope to accomplish the following week." Or they repeatedly revealed that all disagreements within the family were resolved according to the basic family law: "Father isn't always right, but he's

Father," and his word was final with everyone, Olive included, deferring to his way, simply because he was the eldest male in the family. That was hard for most non-Mormon youngsters to swallow.

Somewhere along the way, the Osmonds got a label hung on them: the "Mormon Mafia." Alan was not amused when he heard it, but there wasn't any way it could be erased. All the family could do was to continue along their own path—the one less traveled in those days—and hope that, as Robert Frost promised, it made all the difference in leading a satisfying life.

Olive was the firmest believer that right would triumph in the end. As a mother, she was angered by the changes that had overtaken the American family since the 1950s. And she realized that out in the heartland, away from the establishment press, the Osmonds had many admiring fans. But the establishment press was the most influential and the most liberal, and the Osmonds stood for the past while it was promoting the new morality. To Olive, the promiscuity and morality were major factors in the soaring crime and divorce rates, and, undoubtedly, also sent so many of those free thinkers to the "couch," making psychiatrists happy and very rich! Olive's picture of the world's woes was very simple: "Parents were afraid to discipline their children," she explained, as if that was the simple cause behind the last twenty-five years of distintegrating American values. The breakdown of discipline happened, Olive believed, "because they [parents] thought they were going to hurt their personalities." Her solution? "We're gonna have to get back to the basics—respect for parents, putting the father at the heart of the home where he belongs."

Such eloquence may have been popular with parents and grandparents, but it didn't go over as well with the young, influential crowd dominating the music and television industry. They found it difficult to understand the Osmonds' appeal, but then, the one audience they never could fathom was teenage girls and their mercurial whims.

Television did have one host whose audience reflected the same virtues as the Osmonds. That was Mike Douglas, whose highly successful syndicated talk show rivaled even the mighty Johnny Carson's *Tonight Show* in the ratings. Douglas was as unlikely a candidate for such success as the Osmonds. A former band singer, he was basically rather shy and bland, but he encouraged audience participation, and his audience consisted of ordinary housewives and middle-Americans. Unlike his talk show counterparts, Douglas was based in Philadelphia, away from the jaded New York-Los Angeles crowd.

Philadelphia was great for putting real people in the seats, but it wasn't that easy luring big name guests for the show. It was a long drive to Pennsylvania, and most stars who came to New York on publicity tours had tight schedules. They could lose a whole day getting to and from Douglas' show, a day they could ill afford no matter how big his audience was.

To compensate for the show's location, Douglas offered a unique experience for the stars—not just a few minutes on his show, but co-hosting chores for an entire week. Few stars (many imagine they could be as good as Carson or Cavett if just given the chance), could refuse such an ego-inflating offer. Douglas's viewers were intrigued because it really was nearly impossible to learn much about a favorite star from just a few minutes of prepared stories on the *Tonight Show*. With Mike, stars could discuss their philosophy of life or anything that was near and dear to their hearts—from pet animals, many of which they brought on to introduce to the audience, to pet charities. Stars like Burt Reynolds, Don Rickles, and Kirk Douglas obliged Mike by presiding with him. Most of the stars found it an enjoyable experience, as well as giving them the opportunity to get close to their fans without being pestered.

With ninety minutes to fill, five days a week, Douglas looked for all-around talents who were bright, quick-witted, and interesting. In 1975, Donny and Marie came to his staff's attention. Here were a couple of nice kids with several pleasant songs topping the charts, not acid rock, but melodic tunes that set people's toes tapping. They would be a novelty for Douglas, a change of pace from the older, established, famous faces who usually sat beside him. Teen idols would help Douglas by gaining him a broader audience, too. Best of all, the family came with them. It tied up into a very sweet package. No one could foresee just how successful Donny and Marie would be or how that week would lift their careers.

The audience was delighted with their lively, upbeat tunes, and their warmth and friendliness toward the Douglas studio participants amazed even the host. Unfailingly gracious, Donny and Marie came across as normal teenagers, the sort that appeal to mothers. And when they chatted about their early years and brought out George and Olive for a discussion about parents and teenagers, their casual interaction was appealing. The fact that they were religious was a plus as far as this audience was concerned, but they explained that it was as natural to their lives as eating cornflakes is to millions of Americans. They sang, they danced, they even cooked up a favorite dish in front of the fans. They symbolized what the American family was supposed to be, and their timing was perfect. The Vietnam War was over, and the country was healing its wounds. Watergate had jolted even those people who rarely took an interest in politics; the nation was seeking to restore its values. Donny and Marie epitomized all that was good and virtuous, representing those values of small-town life. Before the week was up, the teenagers had warmed their way into America's heart and had come away with a couple of million new fans.

One new fan was an influential network executive who made a point of spinning his TV dial regularly to see what Douglas was doing. Donny and Marie caught him by surprise. What his network needed to attract a young audience was young performers, and from his critical point of view, these two were savvy enough to win big ratings—and not just from teary-eyed ten-year-old girls.

There were other advantages to hiring the cute brother and sister team. Their reputation for professionalism was well known. The Osmonds never threw tantrums or suffered the kinds of ego trips that ruined other groups. That alone would be a pleasant change from the sudden superstars of the '70s who were forever walking off the set unless their salaries were doubled on the spot, their dressing rooms enlarged into mini-Holiday Inns, and their wives, sweethearts, or relatives put on the payroll. It was enough to give any executive an ulcer—and frequently did.

But the Osmonds were a lovely solution to filling an hour with light-hearted song and dance. Their many gold records certainly merited giving them a TV special, which ABC did late in 1975, just to test their audience appeal. When the ratings came in, ABC signed them to headline their very own weekly show, an hour-long variety format.

Since the special had done so well, Donny and Marie were confident that they could bring in a winner for ABC, which was banking a lot on the two slender teens. When "The Donny and Marie Hour" debuted on January 16, 1976, the duo had the distinction of being the two youngest stars to ever host a prime-time television hour. Donny was eighteen, Marie sixteen, but after all their years in the business, they performed like two old pros.

Although it was Donny and Marie's show, it often featured the other Osmonds, from Wayne, Alan, Merrill, and Jay right down to Jimmy. ABC spared no expense, either, on this extravaganza and allowed them to hire top-name guest stars. Instead of the usual chorus of singers and dancers, the teenagers wanted something truly different. They got it with the Ice Vanities, a chorus of ice skaters who pranced around a rink built in the studio. The kids loved it.

Right from the start, the variety hour built up a strong audience, which made TV critics take notice. Their time slot, Friday nights from eight to nine o'clock, had been deadly to all previous series on ABC since NBC had introduced "Sanford and Son". Redd Foxx and his show practically owned that spot, always scoring in the top ten in the Nielsen ratings. ABC recognized Foxx's star power, but Donny and Marie were a form of counter-programming. Rather than put a similar comedy head to head with "Sanford," they presented a show aimed directly at a different audience and managed to draw off the young people who had been Foxx fans.

Donny, exhibiting the same exuberance he brought to the family's Vegas outings, was a natural-born entertainer. Television did not faze him in the least. Marie, however, was a little more shy around the sound stages at KTLA where the show was filmed. She might never have felt comfortable if not for her big brother. "Donny helped me with everything," she said of those first few weeks on TV. "He taught me to take my time and learn to have fun with what I'm doing. He makes me look good."

To their audiences, of course, Marie was the wisecracker, always taking Donny down a peg. Some of it, Olive revealed, was based on their real-life bickerings. "The two tease each other a bit, but they're pals. They look out for each other," she said.

Every teenager in America with a sibling could appreciate their gentle jibes. And every little sister lived vicariously as Marie continually won the big points. If Marie looked out at the audience and, in reference to their bantering, innocently said, "Actually, Donny and I don't do that in real life," Donny would smirk and say, "Yeah, who ever heard of a kid sister being sharper that her older brother?" To which Marie would sweetly smile and reply, "I did." And that would evoke the line from Donny that became famous: "Cute, Marie, real cute."

And, indeed, they were cute. Cuter than another couple who built their TV fame on verbally baiting each other: Sonny and Cher. Sonny, of course, had literally molded Cher into a star, which, unfortunately, was good for their careers but bad for their marriage. The exchanges between the older couple were much sharper, and filled with double entendres and putdowns about their sex life. Donny and Marie's barbed bantering was gentler. But then, they were luckier because even if Donny had wanted to act like Svengali toward Marie, the family would have stopped it immediately.

Between the ribbings they gave each other, Donny's jokes that Marie seemed barely to tolerate, and the other brothers making their appearances, it turned out to be a well-rounded, family-style series. The most popular spot with the audiences came when Donny and Marie strutted their stuff in their best Vegas style. The costumes were dazzling, there was plenty of flash and splash, and the fifteen-minute segment caught on with all ages. Each one tried to outperform the other, with Marie singing "a little country" and Donny "a little bit rock 'n' roll."

The two teenagers could do no wrong. And they made it all look so simple, as if they just showed up to wing their routines. No one could see the toll the weekly grind took on them (especially Marie, who was always dieting to stay slender for the cameras). The youthful stars often arrived at eight o'clock in the morning for costume fittings and to pick up their scripts. Then there were the scenes to be blocked out so everyone knew where they had to stand at any given moment. Television is an exact medium, with every word timed down to the last second and cameras set to pick up acting in very narrow spots. Anyone off the mark upsets the entire scene and throws the timing off. Crews often work up until the last minute adding material or throwing it out just to hit the running time on the nose. There is little room for mistakes. Of course, a filmed show can always do a retake, but the routines lose their fresh quality and it can be very expensive, so the show was geared to flow from start to finish with few retakes.

Donny and Marie were the Osmonds the fans loved, but their series was a family affair. As usual, the entire clan threw themselves into the show. A professional director was hired, one highly experienced in bringing in variety acts, but the older Osmond brothers took over the producing reins. One Osmond or another supervised avery aspect of the extravaganza, from the writing to the music to the booking of guest stars. They were leaving nothing to chance, and they were careful about the skits and songs.

Alan and Wayne were the actual producers, the ones who watched the pennies and oversaw the sets, writing, and myriad details that go into putting together a weekly show. Merrill was in charge of the fifteen minute concert spot where Donny and Marie soloed and dueted; he chose the music and costumes and put them through their paces during the week, with Jay's assistance as the choreographer.

If any problem arose on the set, most of the time decisions were made on the spot. But every now and again, trouble cropped up that required heavy discussion. On many shows that usually means a lot of hot-headed screaming, so to the production crew, the Osmonds were a pleasant, if somewhat puzzling change from the ordinary. Instead of gathering in a circle and out-yelling each other to resolve differences, the brothers would excuse themselves, go off into a little room for private talks and settle the problem. When they emerged, no one could tell if anyone still disagreed with the decision because once Alan or Wayne gave the order, that was the end of the discussion. Most of the discussions centered around skits or jokes that might be a bit risqué. The Osmonds pored over the weekly scripts with a sharper moralistic eye than any network censor ever did. The writers, of course, learned soon enough what was acceptable and what wasn't. But even then, unless you were a Mormon, you could not always spot trouble!

One writer who has since gone on to perform himself, recalls how the most innocent material could backfire at the last minute. "Once we came up with a skit that we hoped they would like but were afraid that they might find objectionable, since it had Marie playing a biker, complete with black leather jacket and crazy hairdo. But they didn't even blink and we got a go on it. We practiced all week and everything seemed fine until the last day, when we got to the dress rehearsal stage.

"Marie showed up on the set in costume, but there was something missing. We had indicated in the script that Marie was to have this big tattoo on her arm, the way biker's do. That was part of the visual joke, and we were going to have a close-up of the tattoo. Well that brought the brothers down on the stage quickly. They heard us out then disappeared into their private rooms. When they came out a half hour later, they told us, 'No tattoo. As Mormons we are not allowed to decorate our bodies.' We argued for a minute or so, but it was no use.

"That's pretty much the way things went around the show. Nobody was ever unpleasant or anything, but we had very rigid limits. Of course, we did do the skit and it was still funny, but that tattoo on Marie would have been a riot. Aside from the sometimes narrow writing framework, it was one of my nicer experiences in television."

Song lyrics also were closely scrutinized by the whole clan. Donny remembers one then-popular number that called for him to sing a "wine-and-whiskey" line, but he changed it to "milk" and then did a double take to take some of the sting out of what the song lost. Few fans would ever be offended by such words, and lyrics go by so fast that many times it is hard to understand what is being sung, but Donny would have known that he was encouraging certain habits that offended him. As he says, "we do not compromise what we believe in."

Whatever they were doing, it worked. The show gained rating strength as the season progressed, eventually knocking "Sanford And Son" from its top spot. Once again, against the odds and in spite of critical reviews, the Osmonds had triumphed.

Success meant fewer trips home, however, a high price to pay as far as the family was concerned. But since they were reportedly bringing in over $10 million a year from their various enterprises, they felt an obligation to continue as long as possible. It was not all for their personal gain, of course; from the beginning the Osmonds have tithed more than ten percent of their yearly earnings from all sources to the Mormon church, so it was as much for their religion as for themselves that they sacrificed a homelife for their careers.

Besides, while their first love was the farm, Los Angeles was not half bad as far as the teenage singers were concerned. Perhaps Alan, Wayne, and Merrill missed their spacious homes, being family men with children, but Donny and Marie amused themselves with the pleasures a big city had to offer. For Marie that meant lots of shopping. Each of the children now had his or her own apartment in the spacious Westwood apartment house the family owned. It was just a few minutes drive from the studio and walking distance from a couple of California's huge malls full of all the best shops. McDonald's was also nearby, which pleased Donny and Marie, who were junk food lovers, although Olive supervised their visits. The apartment was on a quiet, tree-lined street, far from the glitter of Hollywood, so they were not bothered, although there were always a few fans lingering nearby, hoping for a glimpse of either one. But since they were mostly preteen girls, Donny was their real target. Luckily, Donny appealed to kids from good homes who were well behaved, so they did not mob him on the street. (Of course, they lost all such inhibitions at his concerts where they tried to tear his clothes off!). And no matter how rushed he was, Donny never acted rudely. If he could not stop to sign autographs, he apologized and promised he would the next time.

Another reason they settled in Westwood was because the Mormon church was situated there. When they arrived for the Sunday meeting, the other congregants treated them as members of the group, which was a relief. Their lives really differed very little from those of other middle-class families. To look at them, you would not have known that they were becoming one of the wealthiest families in the country.

They ended their first TV season on a sweet note. Part of Donny's image was his impeccable fashion style, week-in and week-out. He rarely had a hair out of place—until that final show when his brothers rushed out and threw him into the middle of a nine-foot whipped-cream pie. "I think I finally made a big splash on television," he sputtered when he finally freed himself from the slippery mess. And then, with a hearty laugh, he threw whipped cream on everyone else. It was the kind of moment that had made Chaplin and Laurel and Hardy superstars in the old silent films; everyone loves slapstick and everyone wants to throw a pie in someone's face; Donny was acting out his fans' fondest fantasy!

That summer brought the family little rest, though, as they moved on to Nevada to fulfill their Las Vegas contract. Because of the TV show, they had to rearrange the nightclub dates, but they never considered canceling them completely. They would never have intentionally disappointed their fans.

But, all the travel and the stress involved in doing a TV series and concert dates, sometimes with no rest in between, had to take its toll. And their hectic schedule was catching up with the Osmonds—most of all with Marie.

Leaving Vegas one night with their familiar caravan, the older boys looked back and couldn't see the rest of the vehicles. Thinking they had gone a bit too fast, they stopped for a few minutes, waiting for their father and Marie to catch up. When that didn't happen, they turned around and raced back just in time to see an ambulance pull up to an accident scene. Marie had been following George's car and had fallen asleep momentarily at the wheel. George had been slowing down and Marie had slammed into him, totaling her car. She was lucky to come out of it with just some head injuries that healed quickly. But her mother, who was asleep in the back of Marie's car at the time, wasn't as fortunate. Olive suffered several broken ribs and a bruised heart. It really shook up the Osmonds, but not enough to slow them down.

Apparently, Marie also was experiencing dizzy spells off and on, and tests showed that she had a serious potassium deficiency, which is not uncommon in women. But the way Marie drove herself, never getting proper rest, always dieting to look good on TV (which adds ten pounds to everyone onscreen, so that many women try to be slightly underweight before appearing), was endangering her health. Still she pushed on, not only for herself but because the family expected her to.

Then there was Merrill. He had developed a slight heart problem and needed a doctor's supervision. At this juncture, wiser heads might have suggested that the family take the summer off and just relax, but that was not likely. There were contracts to be honored and fans to make happy—that came first. Besides, the family preferred to think of itself as healthy and hearty; sick Osmonds did not make for the right public image. They just kept smiling and offering their upbeat homilies and bore their problems in private.

When they did get back to Utah, George had a wonderful surprise for Marie's seventeenth birthday: her very own palomino. Marie, who loves to ride, was touched and delighted by her father's thoughtfulness.

After a few days in the clean Utah air, the family seriously discussed ways to stay at home more without giving up any part of their careers. George and the older brothers devised a plan to get everyone back home without a cent of lost revenue. In fact, the beauty of their plan was that it actually would increase their profits. The idea was to build their own entertainment complex in Utah, and when they were not using the facilities for TV shows, movies, or recordings themselves, they would rent it out to other entertainers. There were plenty of stars who wanted out of Hollywood, either to get a fresher setting for their programs or because the air was cleaner and the living pleasanter in Utah than L.A. Donny and Marie were at the height of their success, so it looked like a sure-fire moneymaker.

George and Olive, the experts, looked over the available real estate and choose a fifty-two-acre tract in Orem, Utah, right next door to Provo. The family reportedly paid over $1 million for the property and they estimated building costs for the various studios and other buildings would come to another $3 million. It was going to be an expensive undertaking, but the ambitious family was talking about making several movies a year there, and with Donny and Marie's TV show and their yearly flood of recordings, the complex would be in full use the day it opened.

Meanwhile, the senior Osmonds found a beautiful ranch in Provo that they thought could be the perfect home they had always dreamed of owning. In the shadows of Utah's snow-capped mountains, it was 2,000 acres of rivers, streams, trees, and grass. The spread was called Twin Rivers; George and Olive fell in love with it on first sight and bought it. The day was coming, they realized, when the remaining children would be married and living nearby, and they felt this would be the ideal spot to live in contented retirement. Until then, of course, they also maintained the spacious duplex apartment on their other Provo property so that Donny, Jay, Marie, and Jimmy could meet suitable Mormon mates.

A more immediate goal was to get into production for the upcoming TV season. "Donny and Marie" was one of the few mid-season replacement series to be renewed for the fall 1976 schedule. ABC was so delighted with the rosy-cheeked brother and sister that when they learned about the Utah studio, they agreed to transfer the show there when it was finally opened. Until then, of course, the family could still live in Westwood and film the show in Los Angeles.

Though the songsters record sales began tailing off in 1976, and they never regained their gold-record success, it in no way affected their idol status. They were still good looking, talented, and the right age to be fantasy figures, so crowds turned out wherever they toured and their ABC-TV ratings remained strong. The network renewed them for another season.

The Osmond phenomenon was the cause of a greal deal of head shaking within the industry. Their appeal was not quite understood. That may be due to the fact that the majority of moguls measured success and failure purely in terms of New York and Los Angeles, forgetting that the real America was that vast expanse of cities, towns, and hamlets that lay between those two sprawling metropolises. The Donny and Marie fans were the people who attended P.T.A. meetings instead of "getting down" in discos, the ones who frequented church bazaars and pot luck suppers, and whose main entertainment came from the small box in their living rooms and bedrooms. They were the folks who had teenagers and worried about the sex, violence, and drugs that television spewed into their living rooms.

"Donny and Marie" was a welcome alternative, a show the family could watch together. For the kids, there were rock stars like Andy Gibb and Kris Kristofferson, along with establishment stars like Bob Hope and George Burns who appealed to oldsters. Parents did not have to turn away in embarrassment at blue material, and kids could relate to a couple of teenagers neatly handling the responsibilities of their own big-time variety hour. In addition, teenage girls got a kick out of Marie's impatience to be a grown-up eighteen. It reminded them of their own parents' strict dating rules, so they shared something in common with the lovely TV star.

The rest of the family was excited by the biggest project the family had ever dreamed about. The Osmonds never really felt at home in Los Angeles, at least not the boys or

George and Olive. Their dream had been to be successful enough to bring the industry to their port of Utah. And by 1977, their dream was almost realized. In Orem, Utah, there was a groundbreaking ceremony. The Osmonds were building their own studio. And it would prove to be an ambitious project.

Recognizing it for the good publicity event it was, the Osmonds invited the press and public to this great moment in their history. They promised the news media a big show—and delivered. Marie arrived driving a team of Clydesdale horses. It was more like a circus than a construction site as the Osmonds had hired a team of skydivers to perform and provided loads of balloons and a full marching band. Donny came after Marie's horses, driving a bulldozer that officially broke the ground and shoveled the first scoops of dirt away from what would soon be the Osmond movie and television center. But the crowds had come because they knew an airplane was to fly over the area to drop hundreds of pairs of Donny's trademark purple socks down on them. Fifty pairs held certificates that were good for free Marie Osmond albums. It was a great gimmick, but that day, as things sometime happen, the plane missed the construction site and dropped the socks instead in a nearby orchard. Somehow they were recovered and everyone had a grand time.

The grand opening made the wire services, making everyone aware of just how powerful the family had become. No Hollywood press agent could have done better—and by doing it themselves, the frugal Osmonds kept the money in the family.

The Osmonds have never had to worry about being called "big spenders." They are not cheap, but they believe in sound investments over frivolous displays of wealth. And when it came to their studio, they determined that the best way to keep the construction costs under control would be to form their own company and buy the materials themselves and hire whatever help was necessary. It saved them money and enabled them to supervise every step of the operation and keep tabs on the amount and quality of material purchased. It was no more difficult than producing the TV series or their records.

Their policy of low expenses and investing excess cash paid off for them, and none of them ever complained about their life style. It suited their needs. But outsiders who realized just how wealthy they were could not imagine why they didn't live more lavishly. Such nonsense brought no response from the family. They did not impose their choices on others and saw no reason why others should take it upon themselves to make decisions for them. They spent the money where it counted—on their careers.

Even before the giant complex was completed, the Osmonds had plans for its first feature film. They had a script readied for young Jimmy. *The Great Brain* would be reminiscent of Walt Disney's kid-oriented films, a family movie. Alan was alloting $2 million of the Osmonds own money for this venture.

Alan, as the general vice-president of the Osmond empire, second in command only to Papa George, said it was time for them to move into their own productions as Hollywood was no longer providing families like themselves with enough good clean movies that children could see. Many times when the Osmonds wanted to take in a movie, they could find nothing suitable, and this was the void that needed filling. They were not about to go on a crusade to censor or blacklist films that they disapproved of; it was a matter of fair play.

"We're not goody-goody," Alan insisted as he explained their cause to the press. "We're like everybody else. We want good entertainment. . . . There is a lot of sickness, and a lot of quick bucks made on [sex and violence] . . . and we're not going after that." By forming their own movie company, he said, they were going to "help clean up the sickness in the industry." Unfortunately, while Alan and his brothers were so adept at reading the music industry in the '70s, they were novices at their new venture, and that led to some very expensive mistakes. They meant well, but they were just naive about the movie business and moviegoers.

Donny and Marie were used more as shills to get press coverage at events such as this than actual participants in the production company. Their major concern remained the television show, and they were just as pleased to leave the business end to the family.

The lively teens were still the bulwark of ABC's Friday night schedule, so when Marie was about to turn eighteen, the network gave her a special to present what they promised would be the "new Marie." In honor of reaching her majority, and since Donny himself was not going to be a teenager much longer—he would turn twenty on December 9—Marie's special would be the first show to display a more mature look to their entertainment hour. But it would begin with Marie.

The first shock came when it was revealed who was designing a whole new wardrobe for Marie. It was none other than Bob Mackie, the man responsible for giving Cher and other young stars the nude look. Mackie's clothes were very glittery, pure Hollywood, with bare midriffs, plunging necklines, backless, and lots of thigh showing. Mackie, however, also dressed more sedate stars like Carol Burnett and it was this more tasteful look that the Osmonds ordered for Marie.

Marie was thrilled because while they were tasteful, her outfits were also sexy, outlining her shapely curves. Marie may have been tempted, but she was smart enough not to push for anything too daring. To go with her new wardrobe, Marie's hair was reshaped into a softer, more sophisticated style by Suga, a very famous high-fashion hair stylist.

When this "new Marie" debuted, the effect was startling. Olive was amazed by the reaction as little girls across the country rushed out to have their hair cut into the "Marie look." There could be no mistaking her influence on other teenagers. Despite this, the Osmonds' success continued to confound the critics. While more admired variety hours such as "Sonny and Cher," "The Captain and Tennille," "Dick Van Dyke," "Tony Orlando and Dawn," as well as the mighty and beloved Carol Burnett, were biting the dust, Donny and Marie kept rolling along.

At the peak of their popularity, the dynamic duo not only sold records and truckloads of Hawaiian Punch, for which they were the spokespeople, but they moved warehouses full of merchandise, all of it devoted to Donny and Marie, with some fallout for the other Osmonds, thanks to their exposure on the show.

A real Donny and Marie fan had practically a department store's worth of items to choose from. The wide assortment ranged all the way from Osmond posters (Donny, Marie, Donny and Marie, the whole Osmond family, or just the Osmond Brothers and little Jimmy were all available), the same selection of pinup photos and Donny-and-Marie T-shirts, to sheet music and Donny-and-Marie greeting cards with messages like "May Tomorrow Be a Perfect Day." There were wallet photos, charm bracelets, and Donny's famous purple socks—with full-color autographed photos in each one! Or teenyboppers might choose an *Osmond Concert Book*, commemorating a moment they wished they had shared with Donny but couldn't. Just because they couldn't get to his concerts didn't mean they couldn't have a souvenir of one. The Osmonds thought of everything!

For the curious or those lonely fans seeking to find the peace and happiness they envied in the happy family, the Osmonds offered a way for them to find their own fulfillment via the Osmond Family Scripture File, which consisted of 1400 cards with 8,000 comforting thoughts from the Scriptures. This was a highly-recommended product, and the profits from this item were donated to the Osmond Foundation, a non-profit organization that aids the deaf. In the same vein, fans could purchase a book written by Donny himself (with the help of Wayne Hamby) that explained the Book of Mormon. It was titled *Voices from the Dust*. It seems that in his spare moments, Donny often studied the Scriptures, which had led to his authoring the book. And, of course, there was the *Official Book of the Osmond Family*, reliving their inspiring success story.

But the Osmonds did not stop there. Olive, who was really responsible for the mail-order business, her pet project, added a line of fitness equipment for fans who were health buffs. This included the Osmond Family Lifeline Jump Rope and the Lifeline Gym. If that did not grab the faithful, Marie offered her own line of cosmetics, which could be found in stores across the country. They also sold various styles of picture frames. But the best-selling item of all turned out to be Donny Pillowcases. There were thousands of little girls who could not wait to sleep with their heads next to Donny each night.

Two fan clubs were available at five dollars each per year. One was for all the Osmonds and the second was just for Marie, which indicates how her popularity had expanded. There was also a free newsletter that Olive personally wrote each month. Prices for the other items ranged from fifty cents for black-and-white candids to ninety-nine dollars for an Osmond swing bike, just like Jimmy had. Olive did not miss a trick when it came to pasting her popular childrens' faces on items she thought might interest teenage girls. However, she did have her standards. While teenagers love "handsome hunk" pinups of their idols barechested or in neat-fitting bathing suits, the Osmonds allowed no such photos in their catalogue. In fact, Olive went over every photo personally to make sure there was no chest hair sticking out on Donny's photos and definitely no vulgar bulge in full-length photos of the lad. His chaste, antiseptic image was maintained at all times, which did not seem to lessen the ardor of his girlish admirers.

Olive was one of the most anxious of the Osmonds to relocate to Utah full time as she liked to give the family business her undivided attention. Her dream became a reality in November 1977, when ABC approved "The Donny and Marie Show's" move. That started the entertainment complex's TV unit off with a big bang as the series was a six-and-a-half-million-dollar production. With Jimmy primed to begin *The Great Brain*, it looked as if they were going to have their own version of the Disney studio in Utah.

Guests were flown in for the show and put up in Provo. While Marie missed the shopping in Beverly Hills, there were compensations, mainly Brigham Young University.

Now she could meet plenty of eligible bachelors, the kind her parents liked—Mormons.

Donny also was keen on the move. A couple of years before, he had met a shy, pretty Provo girl, and they were getting serious, although this was a part of his life that he hid from his fans. But, like his brothers, he was eager to settle down and start a family. Undoubtedly, the rigid laws regarding sex have more than a little to do with all of these early Mormon marriages, but since they rarely end in divorce, the Mormons may be on to something. Donny did not question the church's laws, and he was willing to wait until he felt ready to make a lifetime commitment. He was just glad he had found the right girl while he was still young.

Of course, until he married, he continued to live with George, Olive, Jay, Marie, and Jimmy, and he never complained about his life under their roof. He was allowed to do pretty much as he pleased, and aside from dating and rehearsing the family act, Donny's main interest still centered around electronics. His room was testimony to his mastery of that science. His fans knew all about Donny's floating bed. He had specially rigged it so that it could be lowered from the ceiling and suspended above his workbench at night when he slept, then raised in the morning so that it disappeared into the side of the wall. Donny's nimble fingers had wired just about everything in the house to respond to buttons; he was a real wizard. And it was a good way for him to relax from his long hours of rehearsal and filming; the family encouraged his hobby.

Right before the family opened their new studios, George and Olive prepared to take a trip they had been planning for nearly a lifetime. Marie was old enough to be left alone in the house (under her brothers' watchful eyes, of course), and the whole family urged their parents to take advantage of the wonderful opportunity that had come their way. So they left on a tour of the Holy Land, an emotion-filled vacation that left them awestruck. Virl, Tom, his wife Lyn, and Jay accompanied George and Olive on their sacred journey. None of them have ever forgotten what they saw and felt as they walked in the footsteps of Jesus.

For Jay, the best moment came when he was actually chosen to give the "sermon" of the day on the very spot Jesus had given his Sermon on the Mount. Words cannot describe the thoughts and feelings that raced through his head when he was so honored. The travelers crossed the Sea of Galilee, waded into the Dead Sea, and saw themselves where the Dead Sea Scrolls were discovered. Olive tried to capture some of the precious moments for their fans in her newsletter, as she wrote of walking the streets of Old Jerusalem and their climbing the same stairs Jesus climbed. But there was so much more. The trip was rich in historic moments. They were allowed to enter Lazarus' tomb and continued into the Garden Tomb where Jesus was laid after his crucifixion.

If ever Olive was grateful for the path her life had taken, for her glorious and gifted family, undoubtedly it was while she stood in these sacred places that she gave thanks for her truly bountiful blessings. Her life so easily could have been less successful. Without their church, George and Olive might have split up before giving their marriage a real chance. And the children might have missed out on all their wonderful adventures if the church also had not encouraged them to stand up and use their God-given talent. They might have just lived quiet, uneventful lives in Utah, happy and close, but they would have missed so much. It was their voices bringing cheer to millions that had made the trip to Israel possible.

The tour also took the group to Egypt, Italy, and the Greek Islands. All of them were properly awed by the Great Pyramid. They toured, climbed, ate, and had a grand time.

All too soon, they were winging home to join the rest of the family for a singing tour and then to start up the new TV season. Olive was thankful that her brood was so successful and busy. She and George must have done something right because now that they were grown up, the kids rarely gave them a bad moment. Donny and Marie had their show, the Osmond brothers kept it running smoothly,

Jimmy was about to start his movie, and Virl and Tom had found an inner peace since finding their own places in the Osmond enterprises.

But there was trouble brewing for the family. Rough times were just around the corner. Once again, there were changes in the record world and Donny and Marie no longer fit the bill.

Record stars go through cycles. For a while, whatever they churn out is grabbed by fans as soon as it comes into the store. Then, just as suddenly, sales taper off, and many of the stars disappear. In a way, that was happening to Donny and Marie. While their popularity was as strong as ever with teenagers and their concerts sold out, and even though their ratings were still high, they were having trouble making the charts. A couple duets, notably "Ain't Nothing Like the Real Thing" and "On the Shelf" hit the Top 100 singles, but the bulk of their income came from other sources. They weren't really worried because they had been through these cycles before. They were more interested in making movies, at any rate, the one show-business area that was still unexplored territory to them.

But it was the same old problem. They were top teen idols, but they received very few movie offers because their moral standards prevented them from considering most modern movie scripts. No one quite knew what to do with them on film. When they were offered something, it was usually by a publicity-wise producer with an eye on the box office and a racy storyline. If an Osmond could be lured into that kind of movie, there was bound to be a big enough scandal to lure crowds to the theater. It had worked before. Pat Boone had frankly admitted he was a fundamentalist Christian when he was a teen idol, but when his career was slipping, he agreed to make what were for him some racy movies to try and save it. The public, of course, had trouble buying Pat as a hard-drinking wastrel, and now he's back singing gospels, drinking milk, and baptizing converts in his backyard swimming pool!

The Osmonds would never shelve their principles and they make that very clear. But when Marie mentioned that she had turned down the movie *Grease*, she created one of the few scandals to ever tarnish their family image. One scandal sheet even accused Marie of out-and-out lying!

It began after the John Travolta/Olivia Newton-John superhit opened and the superstars were on every cover and everyone's lips. One day Marie was discussing her career with a reporter and when the subject of movies arose, she said, "I've been offered some really good parts. *Grease* was one of them. I feel the same way about songs that I do about acting roles. . . . I've refused great songs because they wouldn't change the lyrics." Then she continued and said that when she found the girl's role in *Grease* not up to her principles, the producers agreed to rewrite it for her, but what decided her finally to refuse the role was that "they wouldn't change the other stuff, like the boys dropping their pants. I just wouldn't want my name attached to the picture," she concluded.

There were doubts in some quarters that the part had actually been offered to the pert and popular songbird, precisely because Hollywoodites wondered if teenagers would have accepted her in it with someone like Travolta. But it wasn't until a few months later, when Marie again was quoted as saying, "I was the first person offered the role [in *Grease*]. But for moral as well as professional reasons, I didn't take it," that her remarks were challenged—by the film's producer.

He was kind to Marie but he stated emphatically that Marie was never offered the role because he felt she would not offer enough screen contrast to Travolta. And, indeed, the blond Olivia Newton-John had ended up with the career-making role. The producer did add that this kind of mistake happened all the time. The problem was unscrupulous or naive agents who often tell stars they are up for parts and string them along until the part goes to someone else. He believed that Marie was told she had been offered the role, possibly even given a script since they were always floating around. Certainly he would not brand her a liar, but that did not stop the tabloids from reporting that her statements about *Grease* had brought shame to her Mormon family.

Such reporting was nonsense, of course. The truth is that

Marie had been often mentioned in columns and magazines as a possible co-star for Travolta. Certainly she was the right age and had the right look. If she had been a blonde, there is little doubt she would at least have been offered a chance to read for it.

Marie was growing accustomed to being singled out by the press for the lion's share of exposure. Not all of it was honest or positive, but Marie knew it was impossible to fight such tactics. Women wanted to read about her, and she was a public figure and old enough to be the subject of gossip and innuendo. In a way, it was flattering and another sign of her enormous popularity, although it was a part of the business her family could have done without.

What emerged from the *Grease* episode was a more determined Marie. Whether or not she had been formally offered the part was of no great significance; what mattered was that she had put Hollywood on notice. She wanted to make movies, but on her own terms. "There are an awful lot of parts I'd never dream of playing because of the way we've been brought up," she said. "I'd never do a nude scene—never! And I wouldn't want to be seen smoking or drinking. But we don't need to. People are going back to real family entertainment, and if we can go along with that, we'll do fine."

Marie and her family truly believed that family entertainment was on the way back. They dismissed the fact that the film industry was in the middle of its nudity-and-explicit-sex period. The Osmonds had been faced with dire warnings about their record and television fate if they did not compromise their convictions, but they had won in the end. It was only natural that they would go ahead with their grandiose movie plans convinced that success would follow.

Jimmy was finishing his movie when the other Osmonds flew to Hawaii for their second movie production, *Aloha, Donny and Marie*. It had been scripted for Donny and Marie personally and geared to their teen audience—or so the Osmonds thought! As usual, the Osmonds tied together as many strands of their enterprises as possible: the locale and theme were perfect tie-ins to their Hawaiian Punch commercials, which were saturating the TV airwaves in

1978. The beverage company had sought a youthful image for their fruit drink and felt lucky to have the two teen idols aboard. The Osmonds were excited because it was one of the few drinks not on their no-no list; it may have been laden with sugar, but it had no caffeine, which made it fine to promote. And all the time they were urging teens to "go Hawaiian," Donny and Marie were actually going Hawaiian near Honolulu because their TV show had been renewed for another season. Besides, Donny still had the little girls in his hip pocket; he could go nowhere on the island without having a gaggle of girls trooping after him. Obviously, at twenty, Donny had lost none of his appeal.

The family was very optimistic about their new venture as shooting began. *Aloha, Donny and Marie* was being directed by Howard Morris, one of the original cast members of the legendary TV series "Your Show of Shows." Morris had honed his comedy skills alongside such greats as Sid Caesar and Carl Reiner, not to mention that show's writers, Mel Brooks and Neil Simon. He was an old pro and he captivated his young stars, who put their trust in him.

The film's plot was rather simplistic, or as reviewers would note after it opened, more suitable to a television show than a motion picture. It centered around a brother-and-sister team of entertainers (Donny and Marie, naturally) who come to Hawaii and get mixed up in a net of intrigue. Marie is given an amulet to wear around her neck when she arrives. Unknown to her, the amulet contains the key to a fortune in diamonds, and the bad boys who want it will do anything, including murder, to get possession of it. No one is murdered, of course, but the close calls were meant to have Donny and Marie fans on the edges of their seats. For romance, Donny had what passed for an Osmond love scene. Donny blushed at the mere mention of it, but the actress playing opposite him, a comely blonde, revealed that it was not what she would label a love scene since all they did was come close and then shake hands at the door!

But the real headline-making surprise did not stem from the movie. Donny-watchers were surprised to see him walking around the location holding hands with a very pretty, slender girl who did not seem to be part of the picture. Although she was given a bit part, she did not stay with the cast but with the Osmonds in their Royal Hawaiian Hotel Suite. The look on Donny's face when she was around told the whole story. He was obviously in love with the young lady. When their relationship became public, Donny introduced her as Debra Glenn, who had flown in from Provo to join him on the set. Hawaii presented the right romantic setting he had always imagined would be the background for his marriage proposal. When Debbie said yes, the family could not contain the secret: teen idol Donny Osmond was in love and had set a June wedding date. Many a little girl went to sleep with a shattered heart for weeks after the news broke!

With the engagement announcement came a deluge of requests for more information about Debra. When a teen idol marries, it is news. How had this shy and lovely eighteen-year-old managed to snare one of the most eligible bachelors in America? Donny was happy to oblige.

They had met in 1975 on a double date: Donny's brother Jay was with Debbie and they had arranged a date for Donny. But Debbie said that she had been attracted to Donny from the first moment. "I ribbed and teased Donny," she told reporters. "I was interested in him." Good-hearted Jay did not mind losing his girl to Donny. He preferred to play the field and had shown little inclination to settle down with anyone soon. Donny, more like his other brothers, was only too eager to make the commitment. Debra was fun, easy to talk to, shared his faith, and believed in a strong family unit. She also understood his hidden hopes and dreams and was willing to help him achieve them.

Debra, born in Billings, Montana, had lived in Provo with her parents, Dr. and Mrs. Avery L. Glenn, since she was twelve. Her father was an educator in town, and both Glenns liked Donny. It was true that he was young and so was Debbie, but they were not immature; they understood what marriage meant.

If the Osmonds had any objections, no one could tell from the way they feted the couple. They threw the couple an engagement party luau, a big buffet that ended with a big, thickly frosted cake. Insiders who knew Donny's sense of humor fully expected Debra somehow to wind up with some of it in her face, but her fiancé behaved himself. After all, he had already surprised Debbie once with a pie in her face. They had been courting for a while—long enough for Debbie to appreciate Donny's jokes—when late one night he arrived at her door, rang the bell, and, before she could even get out "hello," heaved a whipped cream pie at her. Instead of being angry, Debbie had laughed, and that seemed to seal their future together.

Within a week of the announcement, the Osmonds and Debbie were back in Provo, supposedly to prepare for the June wedding. But without telling anyone, except the immediate family, they had moved the wedding date up. The secrecy was needed to thwart Donny's fans, who would have mobbed the church on *the* day. To avoid that embarrassing situation, Donny and his former cheerleader fianceé, along with their families, quietly entered the Salt Lake Mormon Temple on Monday morning, May 8, and took their vows. Even though their plans had been known to just the family, (they had not informed the church officials until just hours before the ceremony because they were worried about creating a scene), nearly fifty fans were waiting patiently outside the Temple when Donny and Debbie emerged. No one fully understands how the most zealous fans always know where the idols will be, but Donny's most faithful were not to be denied this moment.

It was a typical Osmond marriage. The newlyweds did not take a normal honeymoon. Instead, the family was scheduled to open a couple of nights later in Las Vegas at the Hilton. So that is where Donny began married life. During the day, the family tried not to disturb the young couple. Anyone attempting to reach the superstar had to go through the switchboard downstairs, and unless callers had the password, Donny and Debby were not disturbed.

Donny did introduce his new bride to the Vegas audiences, and they greeted her enthusiastically, but Debra was not about to join the act. Naturally, people wondered if the couple were planning to have as big a family as the Osmonds. But a press representative for the family said, "probably not. They're planning a medium-size family." Later, the hotel threw them a reception and Debra got her real initiation into America's first family of song.

One Donny fan did more than cry when her hero wed. She did the unthinkable and tried to create a scandal. Stephanie LaMotta lived in New York, and if she had not been the stepdaughter of the "Raging Bull," Jake LaMotta, a former world boxing champion, her story probably would never have made the papers. But all along she had been calling herself Donny's girlfriend and had a photo of them together to prove it. Until then, her story had appeared mostly in the supermarket tabloids that feed on gossip and innuendo. Donny and the other Osmonds denied Stephanie's claims, but she popped up again in the news, this time in more credible publications, claiming that just one week before his engagement to Debra, Donny had flown her to Hawaii to meet his family. After he revealed his engagement news, Stephanie said Donny phoned her "with tears in his voice" to tell her that his family was forcing him to marry a Mormon girl, but that he still loved her.

According to several photographers who had been at the party where Stephanie briefly met Donny, he had been quite polite to the girl, but no more so than he was to all the guests. The party had been a publicity event for the Osmonds on a quick trip they were making through New York. Stephanie, who the photographers said was working for a magazine company specializing in movie magazines, managed to get invited and to get next to Donny when they started snapping photos, which explained the picture she had been flashing of them together. For a few days, Stephanie was news, but the Osmonds followed the family's usual policy and kept quiet.

It was left to Olive a few days after the story had faded away to put an end to any controversy concerning Donny and Debra. Besides the LaMotta gossip, there were rumors to the effect that the Osmonds were not happy that Donny had married so young, that they were afraid it would affect his popularity with the teen market. Olive was very upset that anyone could believe such idle chatter. It was not true, she stated. If anything, the family had taken Debra to its heart. "We believe Donny's marriage was made in heaven," she proclaimed. "It was just meant to be. Donny is mature, very serious-minded and very happy. His bride, Debra, is a lovely thing. . . . She and Donny have the same basic philosophy, and she is very spiritual." Her new daughter-in-law reminded Olive of herself when she was young: like "Mom" Osmond, Debra was interested in education, was a fine seamstress, and had worked in a bank, "so she will be able to balance a check book." She and the rest of the family believed Donny could not have made a better choice for a wife.

Now that Donny was gone from the nest, the house seemed too quiet. Only Jay and Marie were left. Jimmy was Japan's biggest superstar—even more popular than Donny. Nobody could explain why but Jimmy's albums sold like hotcakes in the land of the rising sun, and he was offered his own TV show, which the family urged him to take, even though it meant leaving his close knit clan. Jimmy moved into a family-approved hotel in Japan and flew home as often as possible. Being on his own was a good experience for the son who had been the baby of the family; it helped him become independent and self-sufficient.

Jay, who was the quietest of the bunch, still sang with his brothers and enjoyed his status as favorite uncle, but he still preferred bachelorhood to tying himself down to one girl. He was always taking courses at BYU, which he discovered was a great way to meet pretty co-eds.

That left Marie, who made no secret of the fact that she was looking to get married. She was ready to give up her career, to trade in her Bob Mackie outfits for maternity clothes if Mr. Right came along. "I look forward to getting married and having babies," she said. But with eight protective brothers checking out her boyfriends, Marie's love life was rather limited.

In Hollywood, Marie went the glamour route, dating such handsome macho men as Dirk Benedict and John Schneider. Whenever she was with a handsome young star, the gossips would have her married the next day. As wise as she was to the price stars pay for their fame, Marie was bothered by what her media image did to her love life. "It's hard for a guy to call me," she often sighed. Thus, Marie depended on her brothers, especially Donny, to get her dates, saying, "If I see someone I like, I tell Donny. He calls the guy and says 'How'd you like to go out with Marie?'" No one ever said no, it was just getting them to understand that, offstage, Marie was a normal girl.

Of course, before he would let the guy know Marie was interested, Donny had to approve of him. He liked to joke, "A guy should know five things before he dates Marie—they are Alan, Wayne, Merrill, Jay, and me." And he wasn't entirely kidding. Her brothers have always influenced Marie in her thoughts, dress, career, and private life.

Their main influence was to motivate Marie to carry on with her career and to help broaden the family's business base. When they realized how much Marie's style was copied by little girls, they went right into action packaging her line of cosmetics to be sold in K-marts across the country. K-mart was chosen for a very sound marketing reason: Marie's fans were little and not ready to spend the kind of money personal care products cost in department stores. The K-Marts were priced right for the lower middle class, the kids who bought the most.

Olive, too, developed a new line of Osmond merchandise. Inspired by Bob Mackie and the other designers who helped make over the "new Marie" at eighteen, Olive went back to her first love, fashion design. Butterick Patterns, one of the biggest and best pattern companies, which was always on the lookout for new designers with a feel for the youth market, backed a line of Osmond clothes. "Olive's Kids," as the line was named, got a splashy introduction in the New York's fashion trade press. Rather than just include the designs in a catalogue, the company hosted the kind of event usually reserved for Calvin Klein or Ralph Lauren. But then, the models were none other than Donny and Marie.

The fashion show was held in the New York, New York disco, where Olive explained how her seventy-five-piece sportswear line had begun. Way back, when she and George were just starting out, Olive revealed she had "run a little dress shop in Ogden." It was there that some of the salesmen noticed that Olive had an uncanny knack for picking out items for her shop that invariably became best-sellers. Soon, she modestly admitted, "The salesmen would come in with their samples and have me pick out the dogs. I was good at that. Then they would take the rest of their collection on into town and sell it."

"Olive's Kids" offered something for everyone, from young men to junior misses and children's sizes, and they were sold at Sears and other moderately priced stores. Plans called for winter and summer lines with Olive overseeing everything. Marie, too, would shortly have her own line of clothes, in soft, feminine fabrics and with youthful lines.

That year, the family worked non-stop. There weren't enough hours in the day for all their projects. From the fashion debut, they went to Las Vegas and then back to Hollywood for their new TV season. There were, however, a few cracks beginning to appear in their success story.

Jimmy's *Great Brain* movie was in trouble and would never get a wide American release. Most exhibitors were wary about booking it, finding it very old-fashioned, the kind of movie that did not bring audiences running. *Aloha, Donny and Marie*, which had been retitled *Goin' Coconuts*, opened to generally bad reviews and disappeared quickly from theaters. And, as if that wasn't enough, their show began to slip in the ratings. Was it coincidence that their popularity fell drastically right after Donny's marriage? It had happened before, to nearly every young star catapulted to idoldom; as soon as something as real as a wife comes in, kids' fantasies are turned elsewhere. Some teen stars deliberately wed so they can move on to mature roles. That was not Donny's motive, but the results were the same.

ABC gave Donny and Marie every chance to succeed. They moved the show from Friday nights to Sundays and slotted it an hour earlier when the young kids were still watching. It was renamed "The Osmond Family Show" and the other brothers participated more. Nothing worked. The last show aired in May 1979.

After the last hour, the family sat down to appraise their

situation. Apparently the Donny and Marie duo had lost its popularity with the fickle fans. In analyzing the problem, they decided that now was a good time to separate their careers. They were going in different directions, anyway, and with Donny a married man, a lot of the old teen-style jokes would not work anymore. Both Donny and Marie also wanted to act, and if they wanted producers to accept them, they had to create unique and separate images. However, they would still sing together with the Osmond Brothers in Las Vegas and on the extended tours they made every summer.

Marie found the challenge of being on her own exciting. It was the first step away from her brothers, and she approached it tentatively, until an offer came along that bolstered her confidence, convincing her that maybe she could be an important star.

5

Marie Makes a Big Mistake

After nearly a lifetime of living in her brothers' shadows, Marie was looking forward to forging her separate identity. The split from Donny would give her the freedom to explore new challenges and to emphasize her own lively personality. She had a new mission: to be accepted in the acting fraternity as a serious actress. Donny, too, looked forward to adding acting to his list of accomplishments. They had to agree that their first outing in *Goin' Coconuts* did little for their acting ambitions, but at least they had gained some on-camera experience.

Both of them, however, had family commitments to fulfill. One of their yearly tours was about to begin; the family act still was popular in Las Vegas and around the country, although its popularity was waning somewhat in Europe. The audience was comprised mainly of young girls and their parents, people who had grown up with the Osmonds and wanted their kids to enjoy a nice family experience.

Marie was the main attraction. She had grown into a pretty, pert, and good-natured young woman, the kind young girls admire and hope to emulate. Over the years there have been few female idols. Television has had its share of popular teen stars, but nobody ever wanted to cut her hair to look like Kristy McNichol, no matter how talented an actress she is. That kind of adoration is reserved for women who lead glamorous lives and do something out of the ordinary. Dorothy Hamill was idolized after winning the gold medal for figure skating at the Olympics, a feat teenage girls could fantasize about. Suddenly, little girls were turning out in record numbers in skating rinks, wanting to be like Dorothy.

Marie engendered the same kind of excitement. Because her family made her follow strict dating rules and regulated her life, other girls sympathized with her. Usually Hollywood teenagers who reach stardom are photographed in evening gowns with young tuxedoed escorts from the day their first movie is made, but Marie was not permitted to live life in the fast lane. Her fans lived vicariously with her as she awaited her sixteenth birthday, when she was allowed to go on her first date. From then on, her every move was the subject of gossip and speculation.

For a short time Marie dated Dirk Benedict, the handsome young star of a favorite teen TV show, "Battlestar Galactica." They met when Dirk came to Provo to film a "Donny and Marie" show. They even made the rounds in Hollywood, attending glamorous parties and premieres, something Marie had not been allowed to do before. It was all terribly exciting for her. But she was keeping a little secret from her fans. While the flashbulbs popped to capture Marie and Dirk holding hands, and magazines sought her advice for other young girls, she was really living two lives. She had met a boy in 1977 and was getting serious when duty came between them. Now he was back, and Marie was making wedding plans.

In the accepted way, Marie had met Jeff Crayton through mutual friends. He was tall and boyishly handsome. In some ways, he looked like an Osmond, especially when he flashed his dimpled grin. Marie liked him instantly. As for Jeff, he could not get the dark-eyed girl out of his dreams. He followed her around the BYU campus, where she was auditing courses and he was enrolled. One teacher told him her class was full, but Jeff still sat at an empty desk, just to be near the object of his affection.

It would be hard for any girl's head not to be turned by such attention. Jeff won Marie's. One April Fool's Day, she gave him an unforgettable demonstration of her affection. She surprised him with a pie in the face!

The Osmonds had nothing against Jeff, but they did feel Marie was too young for a serious romance, so when Jeff was called to do his two-year mission work in 1977, they were relieved. For two years Jeff lived in Spain where he was allowed but one letter a week from Marie. Mormons on missionary work are not permitted to pursue personal ambitions, either professional or romantic; they must dedicate themselves to the people and tasks at hand with no outside distractions.

But in spite of their two-year separation, Marie and Jeff still had strong feelings toward one another, so strong that Marie met Jeff at the airport the day he returned from Spain. Obviously, they were still in love.

Donny and Marie were then winding up their final ABC shows, and Jeff was a frequent visitor at their Orem studios. Nobody realized how far the romance had progressed until one day when Jeff came to pick Marie up. As he later told the newspapers, ever since the day "Marie surprised me with a pie in the face . . . I have wanted to get even with her. So I called her out of rehearsal yesterday and I told her to close her eyes and that I had a big surprise, and I got her in the face with a banana cream pie."

Marie was still recovering from that surprise when Jeff got down on his knee to propose to her. When Marie said "yes," Jeff slipped a one-carat diamond ring on her finger, and they announced their engagement to the press on Memorial Day, 1979. The wedding, they said, would be in August, when Marie returned from an Osmond tour.

As things turned out, it was fortunate that Marie, unlike Donny, did not rush into a hasty marriage. But then, it was easier for the Osmond boys to wed because men are called upon to be the breadwinners in the family while the women make the home. They had always recognized that, for Marie, marriage would be a complex problem. She would have to sacrifice her career while the brothers continued theirs without a hitch. Could Marie do it? Or would she find a way to combine both? No one could say for sure until she was actually married.

Right from the start, problems sprang up between Marie and Jeff. Her family said very little, but there was a feeling that they did not entirely approve of the upcoming union. Most of the problems stemmed from Marie's constant traveling, which would put a damper on any relationship. Jeff could not ignore the priorities Marie had; her family was more important than their relationship, or so it seemed to him. Actually, Marie was fulfilling her commitments, the way she was raised to do.

The engagement went from bad to worse as the couple took a good look at their future. She and Jeff called the wedding off, although she said nothing about it publicly until she was signing autographs in Montgomery, Alabama, where the family was entertaining on the Fourth of July, and she was asked about her wedding day. There and then she admitted the engagement was over. She offered nothing more than to say that "mutual differences" had arisen and the decision was a joint one. She implied that she and Jeff would still see each other.

But they did not, which Jeff later complained about. Clearly upset by the turn of events, Jeff insisted Marie was still in love with him but her family had interfered, fearing they would lose her from their act. Such charges stung the Osmonds, but they tried not to retaliate in the press.

Sticking to their original explanation, they waited for the unpleasantness to die down. Still Jeff persisted with his public outrage. "I think one day I'm going to pick up a paper and read that Marie has collapsed and badly damaged her health," he said angrily. And, indeed, shortly after she broke the engagement, Marie did wind up in the hospital for exhaustion. This was a periodic pattern with Marie who, due to her poor diet and relentless schedule, suffered from dizzy spells. Most of it was tied in with her potassium deficiency, but she was more concerned with her figure than her health, thus the repeated hospital visits. According to Jeff, however, all Marie really wanted was "love, a home, and a family. If her family would let her, she'd walk away from her career tomorrow." He recalled watching the songstress drive herself when she was ill and near collapse, all of which he blamed her family for allowing to happen.

It was not until months later that Marie finally offered her side of the story, and only in the hope that it would put a stop to Jeff's pot shots at her family. Completely denying that her family had ever said a word against Jeff or that they compelled her to continue working, Marie claimed the trouble began right after the engagement when Jeff pressured her to quit her career. He wanted her to give up her work so the two could concentrate on his. (He was an aspiring singer/actor.) Marie tried to explain to Jeff that she had at least a year's worth of contracts to honor, but according to her, Jeff would not even listen. It was at this point that Marie realized if she married Jeff, as an obedient Mormon wife, she would have to obey him if he ordered her to give up her career. Liberation has not come to Mormon women. The husband is the absolute head of the house. As Marie saw it, in a good marriage, couples discuss problems as they arise and work them out in harmony, which is how the senior Osmonds have always worked it. If she wanted as equally happy a coupling, Jeff might not be the right man, and that is when she decided she wanted out. She revealed that she was shocked by Jeff's "me-me-self-self-self attitude," which she felt would lead to "conflicts and mutual heartache and sad children."

Marie's breakup was good news to the Hollywood bachelors who had been left in the lurch by her engagement. Besides Dirk Benedict, rock star Andy Gibb was also making headlines with his love for Marie. Nothing ever came of that, of course. The problem was not that Andy had been raised in another religion, but that he did not have a life style compatible with that of the Osmonds. Still speculation about a romance with Andy raged for several months.

There was little time for Marie to shed tears over her broken romance, however. The Osmond Brothers felt it was time to wind down their participation in the performing end of the business. The crowds really had come out to see Donny and Marie, and the youngsters were looking to expand into movies and more TV, which would leave little time for concert tours. Besides, the older brothers were establishing themselves behind the scenes in the business end of their entertainment industry. Most of the year was spent in Provo, experimenting with their recording studio, trying out new sounds, trying to attract other acts to rent the equipment. The transition had gone smoothly.

Alan, under George's supervision, was the general vice-president who watched over everything. Merrill ran Osmond Productions, which included the entertainment center for TV and movies as well as the Osmond museum and hotel they had in the planning stages. Wayne was in charge of the Kolob Music division, which was the Osmond record company. The two recording studios and the music publishing arm were under his wing as well as the division responsible for the educational records to aid reading, which the Osmonds produced and distributed. Jay handled all the details for any Osmond tours. Their Osbro Concerts company was set up to book the family into concert halls and arenas. Virl and Tom took care of all the administrative work for the fan clubs and made the merchandising agreements. They also managed the actual plant facilities in Orem. Jimmy was in Japan most of the time, doing his TV show. When he was home, it was to tour with the family and pitch in wherever he was needed. Donny and Marie were still the mainstays of the concert tours.

In 1980, Alan and his brothers announced that the Osmonds would be making their farewell tour as the act America had come to love. They were booked solidly throughout America and in the countries where they had always been highly popular.

First they played Las Vegas and were as big a draw as ever. The Osmonds, with their flashy choreography, solid harmonies, and show-biz savvy, knew how to turn a hip audience on in places like Vegas. But once they left the States, they faced serious and embarrassing problems.

They did not expect to be swept up by the same Osmondmania of the '70s when they arrived in London, but the total lack of interest in their tour was a shock. There was something sad in watching the large entourage arrive to play to nearly empty halls throughout England. All the wives and children were along, and even under the best of circumstances, such a large group traveling on one bus, even one as well-equipped as the Osmonds, often gets cranky.

They were obviously tired and depressed as the tour continued. Driving all night, Marie often had to stretch out on the floor when she wanted to nap, with everyone stepping gingerly around her. Donny, Debby, and Donny Jr. cuddled together in two seats with the baby nestled in Donny's arms. The schedule was as exhausting as ever and they didn't have the "up" of screaming fans to lighten their heavy hearts. Alan admitted the tour was frustrating and disappointing because "we came to wave goodbye; but nobody waved back."

From Manchester, England, reports filtered back to America that the Osmonds actually had to call on their Mormon brethren in that town to paper the theater so they could give their concert. The Osmonds denied doing so but added that they had given away some 500 tickets as a nice gesture to the Mormons there. It was obvious that the day of the Osmonds was definitely over in England.

The long hard gruelling hours, haphazard meals, and lack of sleep took a big toll on Merrill. The Osmonds had a very scary moment when they thought they might lose him. As they drove into London, Merrill was wearier than the others. His son Shane was hospitalized with a suspected case of meningitis. This was on top of Merrill's rarely-discussed heart problem, which had troubled him for years. It was too much for him; he collapsed at their hotel. The family was very frightened as he was rushed to the hospital. But in the finest Osmond tradition, Merrill rose from his sick bed and went on with the others that same night. He was driven dramatically to the theater in an ambulance and while he performed, a nurse stood by backstage with oxygen tanks just in case.

Once again, Alan and Wayne and the others had timed their career decision right. The Osmonds were finding it increasingly hard to book themselves into good arenas. But, Alan promised, the fans had not seen the last of them yet, just the last of the old Osmond act. "We'll pursue solo careers," he promised. "We finally decided it was time for all of us to stretch our talents a bit and try a few things on our own." Besides, Alan added, with the current inflation, "It's gotten too expensive to keep the group together."

Was this to be the end of America's First Family of Song? Not by a long shot. The Osmonds are just too shrewd ever really to quit, not as long as there is money to be made and people to make smile!

6

Marie Spreads Her Wings

As the new decade began, the Osmonds' careers were in turmoil. Donny, married and with a child, no longer interested teenage girls. The older brothers had been mere backups in the act for nearly ten years. Jimmy never had caught on in America. Only Marie maintained her great popularity.

There were rumblings that the slender, pretty singer really wanted out of the business, to find a husband and retire from the limelight. Not only was she in constant danger from her mineral deficiency, but she also had an ulcer, just another signal that, despite Olive's statements that none of the children was ever pushed, Marie certainly was under more stress and strain than is healthy for a twenty-year-old girl.

But the worst problem was the drain the entertainment complex had become on their finances. Built at the height of Osmond popularity, once their show was cancelled the studio was rarely used. Alan, Wayne, and Merrill were in fevered conversation with several cable TV companies, trying to work out a deal to bring either cable shows or syndicated series to Orem, but they generated little interest. Meanwhile, the facilities had to be maintained at a high level, which was costly.

The truth was, even if Marie had wanted to retire, she could not while the family faced financial setbacks. She was the only Osmond getting big money bids from the industry.

Fred Silverman, the Osmonds' old boss from their ABC days, approached Marie with an offer she could not refuse. Marie's loss of the show with Donny had not dampened her popularity, at least not according to the indications of the I.Q. ratings. These ratings are far more important to network executives nowadays than even the Nielsens as the I.Q. rates how stars score as identities with the public. Before series are cast, the names of probable stars are run through the computer to see how high their individual popularity quotient is. The higher the I.Q., the better the chance of getting a series. Marie's score was very high and Silverman wanted her for his newly adopted network, NBC.

Silverman had come to NBC with a great deal of fanfare, hailed as that network's "savior." NBC had been third in the overall network ratings for so long even its stable of stars made it the butt of their jokes. Silverman was the magician who had made CBS number one in the '60s, been hired away by ABC in the '70s, and took that network from number three to number one by buying such comedies as "Happy Days" and "Laverne & Shirley." At the time, ABC had been the butt of industry jokes. Now NBC was banking on his programming genius to shoot them to the top again. But his first season had been a disaster. What he needed was a sure-fire winner, and he hand picked Marie Osmond as one of the stars who would bring NBC a young audience. He put her under exclusive contract, a multi-million dollar pact that included her own series and several TV movies.

Marie was thrilled. Here at last was the chance she had been waiting for. And the other Osmonds approved the deal because Marie would make the movies under the family's production banner. Would there be some changes in the Osmond attitude toward movies now? That question intrigued Hollywood, which wondered how many modern movies would meet the Osmonds' strict moral code. "I wouldn't play a prostitute because I wouldn't feel right about it," Marie had said. And even with the family having cash problems, they would not compromise their values at any price.

Rather than search for a modern script, the Osmonds turned backward for Marie's first television movie. The budding actress had always admired a short story by O. Henry, a Christmas tale that in a few strokes seemed to sum up the true spirit of the holiday—and of life. In the Bible, that first Christmas night when the baby Jesus lay in his manger in Bethlehem wrapped in swaddling clothes, there appeared the magi, three wise men who had traveled over fields and streams to bring gifts to the newborn King of Kings. Those gifts were of gold, frankincense, and myrrh, but they realized they were of no more value to the little babe than the gift of love, which was all the other poor peasants could bring to the stable. O. Henry recaptured that spirit of love in his "Gift of the Magi," a tale of two terribly-in-love but impoverished newlyweds who sell their most precious possessions to buy each other a special gift for Christmas. Marie played the wife who sells her luxurious hair to buy her husband a gold chain on which to display the gold watch his father had left him, and which he cherishes above all else—except, as it turns out, his wife. Timothy Bottoms portrayed the husband who has sold that same gold watch the night before Christmas to buy Marie an expensive comb and brush set for the hair she considers her crowning glory. That Christmas, both learn that material possessions mean little. and love is the greatest gift.

The Osmonds did not update the story but did retitle it "The Gift of Love," so that no one could mistake the message. Besides hiring the high-priced Timothy Bottoms, no expense was spared, and another Hollywood star was brought in to co-star with Marie—James Wood who had won acclaim and an Oscar nomination for *The Onion Field*.

Marie threw herself into the project, seeing it as a test and a showcase to attract a new audience. While she did not put down modern movies, agreeing that sex has its place in people's lives, she also believed "there is a need for family entertainment." And while she said, "I don't see anything wrong with the belief that the human body is beautiful, what's inside is important too."

Making the movie was exciting, too. "There are a lot of firsts in this project for me," Marie said. "I've never done straight drama before. I have only one brief singing number. And I'm playing a married woman for the first time."

The night the show aired, Marie had butterflies in her stomach. Often, dedicated actors throw themselves into projects and get so caught up in them that it is hard to judge for themselves how successful they are. Reviewers, of course, cannot be swayed by good production values or intentions. Viewers depend on their objectivity to choose between an evening's many choices. In the last ten years, the Osmonds had rarely been well received by record or TV reviewers, but Marie, the novice actress, could not be disappointed in what was said about her performance. While they were not raves, they also were not pans. The *Los Angeles Times* critic noted that Marie was still exhibiting "too many toothy Osmond grins," but he added, "there is grace, poise and a subtlety of emotion in her performance. She isn't quite ready to take on Lady Macbeth. But this is a very good start."

At that stage in her acting career it was encouraging praise. It helped build her confidence for the other projects on the drawing board. Marie's contract also meant that money was flowing into the family and the entertainment center was open again.

When the movie was completed, the Osmonds moved ahead with plans for Marie's TV series. Television productions had gotten so expensive that most new shows were booked, at first, on a tentative schedule of four to six weeks to see if they could build an audience. That was Silverman's plan for Marie's hour variety specials. She was given four weeks to see what she could do.

Silverman put a damper on the family enthusiasm, however, when he also decreed that the hour would have to come from NBC's Hollywood studios, not from the Osmond entertainment complex, at least for these first shows. Undoubtedly, if they were successful, Marie could ask for and get the moon. But Silverman was keeping a sharp eye on expenses, and it added too much to the production costs to fly stars to Utah.

If her brothers were disappointed at that directive, Marie did not bat an eye. In fact, she was pleased, as she liked Hollywood more than the rest of the family. And she caused quite a stir when she opened up for once in an interview about her life and her family. Claiming she was on her own for the first time while making her "Marie" series, she chattered on: "I'm the black sheep of the family. I've been making my own decisions since I was fourteen. I'm not a little airhead with no opinions, bowing to the mighty Osmond court in the sky." Clearly, the Osmond image was beginning to bore Marie, who was the most sophisticated and outgoing of the clan.

But when her candid comments made it back home, a shocked Olive gave an interview of her own and pointed out that Marie most definitely was not living alone in California; Mom was there as usual. If Marie was reaching for the sophisticated crowd that dismissed her as an Osmond robot, Olive would have none of it. Once again, Marie was subdued and went back to work for the good of the family.

Marie's hour was lavishly produced and the guest list was impressive, but the ratings were not good. Part of that, no doubt, was due to lack of interest in Marie Osmond, but the root cause of its failure was more likely because variety hours were considered dead on television. And, of course, the show was on NBC, where series consistently scored lower than on the other networks. The young star did learn a few lessons from that show, though. First, she learned that until the day she wed, her mother would be her constant companion. And she found out how insecure most female stars are about themselves.

For years Marie had suffered from an inferiority complex. It began when she was traveling with her brothers and fighting what was then a losing battle with her weight. And she had an overbite that required dental work. Even though her teeth were now perfect and her body all womanly curves, Marie said she felt inferior standing next to Raquel Welch or Jaclyn Smith on her show. Both ladies are indeed Hollywood beauties, but Marie got a lift when she learned that these women were just as insecure and that many female guests balked at standing next to Marie because they were envious of her slim 22" waist.

It was an eye-opener for her. But nothing could ease the pain of another cancelled series. After years of success, working hard and coming up a loser was a bitter pill, not just for Marie but for all the Osmonds. But they swallowed hard and smiled through another bad time; their positive attitude helped Marie.

The series was gone, but she still had a couple of movies to look forward to. For *I Married Wyatt Earp*, Marie traveled to Old Tucson, Arizona, and environs, the actual location where Earp had roamed in the late 1800s. This was somewhat racier material than Marie usually accepted, although the kissing was still quite chaste. As the widow of the legendary U.S. Marshall Wyatt Earp, Marie had an important part in this, the last chapter of the wild, wild west when Earp had his showdown at the O.K. Corral. Handsome Bruce Boxleitner co-starred as Earp, one of two men vying for her attention. The major problem with the script, as far as the Osmonds were concerned, was that Earp was a married man when he fell in love with Josephine Marcus, (Marie), a singer passing through Tombstone who decides to stay when she spots Earp. Naturally, after a lot of action and a little romance, Earp and Josie live happily ever after in this light-weight entertainment.

Marie was excited about the project because it gave her both singing scenes and several dramatic acting moments. NBC was decidedly less excited after screening the project, and they shelved it for over a year. When it finally aired in January of 1983, the reviews were mixed. The *Hollywood Reporter*, an industry trade paper, called it "unconvincingly antiseptic. . . . The emphasis on somewhat corny romantic twists neglects to generate much suspense for the action sequences." Of Marie's performance, the reviewer merely said, "Osmond limns a charming portrait of a city-bred gal who falls for a famed lawman, but her acting range is still erratic and limited." Boxleitner fared little better. He "cuts a dashing figure, but his clenched-teeth performance is one-dimensional," was the reviewer's appraisal. Fortunately, in a much more widely-read and listened-to publication, *TV Guide*, reviewer Judith Crist was kinder to one and all. "Marie Osmond has some good moments in *I Married Wyatt Earp*," Crist reported, and overall, she found that "there's never a dull or unromantic moment" in the production. Again the ratings were respectable if not spectacular.

But the project that came closest to Marie's heart was the movie version of her own parents autobiography, *Side By Side*, which depicted the struggles the family had endured on their way to becoming singers on Andy Williams' show. What made it so intriguing was that Marie was not playing herself, but starring as Olive, her own mother. Joseph Bottoms, brother of Timothy, with whom Marie had co-starred in "The Gift of Love," played George Osmond.

Filming the movie was sometimes very eerie for Marie. One scene in particular stood out, the one in which Olive finally has a daughter. "I have never done anything freakier than acting out giving birth to myself," Marie said of the project. "To be standing there as my mother and holding me in my arms—it was a feeling impossible to describe."

When the movie was over and screened for the family, Olive and George cried through most of it as memories of moments they had long ago buried came rushing back. Marie appreciated anew the dedication and devotion her parents had given her and the boys, and she realized the sacrifices they had made so that the children could have the best of everything. Without show business, their lives most probably would have been very ordinary. But because of the elder Osmonds, they had known excitement, had sung for kings, and shopped in London, Paris, Rome, and cities around the world. They had been given an extraordinary childhood. If there were tiny regrets over missing out on dances and girlish confidences with close friends, they were overlooked when, as adults, they mingled with the top stars in the world. Outside their studios in Orem was a large wall constructed just for guest stars to leave their handprints, à la the famous Graumann's Chinese Theater in Hollywood.

And they had the cream of show business immortalized there, from Bob Hope and George Burns to Andy Gibb and Kris Kristofferson.

Marie could recall the sensation of celebrating New Year's twice in one day. The Osmonds had been singing on an Asian tour when they returned home on New Year's Eve. They left after celebrating the event in Asia, and flying home they crossed the international dateline, which allowed them to celebrate again in America. How many people had such memories?

Or birthdays like Marie's. There was the time she had been pushed into a huge pie to celebrate her special day by Sonny and Cher, with whom she was guesting. Her sixteenth birthday brought greetings from a planeload of fellow passengers. In the middle of the flight, the captain came on the loudspeaker and announced there was a special passenger aboard, Marie Osmond, and he asked everyone to serenade her with "Happy Birthday," which they did with gusto. On her seventeeth birthday, Marie had received a palomino pony from George, a gift she cherished because it was exactly what she had wanted. And for her eighteenth birthday, she had received her new Bob Mackie wardrobe, her Suga hairstyle, and a new image thanks to her TV show. Those were the very moments other teenagers envied just as she sometimes envied their lives filled with friends and parties. But she knew she would not trade places with any of them.

Side By Side made the family laugh and cry and remember much of their good and bad sides. Marie felt privileged to be a part of the movie.

Meanwhile, she and Donny had reunited for an extraordinary event themselves. The whole clan was invited to President Reagan's inauguration, where Donny and Marie did them all proud as the closing act for the official Inaugural Ball, the one that was attended by President and Mrs. Reagan. The Osmonds had been Reagan supporters all the way, lending their time and talents to fund raisers among young party members. So it was only fair that the ball's organizer, Frank Sinatra, put them on the entertainment bill. And their patriotic songs brought down the house, not to mention the excitement they brought to tens of millions of Americans as the festivities were turned into a TV spectacular.

With all this activity, it was no surprise that Alan, Wayne, Merrill, and Jay were starting to miss the business. The tours, the applause, the sense of working together—it all gets into the blood, and the four original Osmond brothers were the ones who had loved it the most, who never felt cheated of a childhood because they were on the road.

Up in Orem, they felt there was something missing. Being with their families was pleasant, especially since they all—except Jay, the perennial bachelor—had growing children. But their dad was often with Jimmy in Japan, and Donny and Marie spent time on the road with their many projects, leaving an empty spot that the Osmond enterprises could not fill. They all lived within five miles of one another, just as Alan had suggested, and they spent most nights visiting each other, which gave them the opportunity to explore new musical ideas. They still got the trade papers and kept up with the latest trends.

What had caught their interest recently was the way gospels and country music had crossed over into the pop field. Disco was dead on the charts; hard rock had given way to upbeat, rhythmic numbers, the type that were Osmond specialties. And, after all, they had cut their teeth on gospels. They began to fool around with their style in the studio, which offered ample equipment to try anything. Their favorite country act was the Grammy-winning Oak Ridge Boys, who proved that style had become supreme even in country.

When they had locked up the sound they liked, the quartet arranged to rent time at the FAME studios in Muscle Shoals, Alabama. Since they were getting back in the business, they followed their father's maxim: "Hire the best," which is why they did not just turn out a record from their own facilities. They were still novices with this sound and style. In Muscle Shoals, they hired the best musicians around, importing some from Nashville, and came up with a single that hit the Top 30; their next single made it to the

Top 20. The Osmond Brothers were back on the charts! But what was more exciting was being named winners of an award as the "New Country Singles Act" of 1982, given by the bible of the music business, *Billboard*.

Suddenly, they were the hottest act in country. And they knew better than to sit back and wait for success to happen. They moved quickly, getting out an album of country songs and working up a new act. In the act, they spoofed their early years as child stars, and they emphasized their musical versatility by playing every instrument in their repertoire, from saxophones and drums to banjos, fiddles, and trumpet.

Best of all was the fact that they had at last vindicated the Osmond Brothers. They had long been considered mere backup singers to their flashier siblings, Donny and Marie, and record companies had not listened very seriously when they considered moving into this new area. So the brothers had backed themselves and won the bet.

Donny and Marie were as thrilled for their brothers' success as anyone. It had been a little sad leaving them in Utah while they continued their careers. Now the family could get together again, and their renewed success also gave the Osmond Brothers a spirited new confidence that reinforced their efforts to hold onto their entertainment complex, which some were calling the "Osmonds' white elephant."

7

Donny Gives His Regards to Broadway

While Marie was struggling with her acting career and Alan, Jay, Merrill, and Wayne were rebuilding their singing act, Donny hit the road. Since their marriage, he and Debbie rarely had been able to spend any real time in their Provo home. Luckily, he had explained his career carefully to Debbie, so she understood. Even after the arrival of Donny Jr. in 1979, and Jeremy in early 1981, she was willing to live out of a suitcase.

Donny, like Marie, was struggling to sustain his career. He was doing it partially for the family, which had finally decided to sell off its distribution company since all the products they had originally scheduled were not forthcoming. But Donny was also doing it for himself. After twenty years in show business, it was all he really knew. To be sure, he amused himself with electronics (and had devised many of the Osmonds' special effects when they were together), but that was a hobby. Singing was his life. Besides, he, too, had to prove that the Osmonds and their principles could survive, that they were not just cute kiddie stars with no real talent.

Since the career split from Marie, Donny had not been

very active; he had made a TV movie, *The Wild Women of Western Gulch*, with Joan Collins, but he had not received very much publicity for that, nor did he get other offers as a result of the movie.

Other teen idols have experienced similar career lulls. In fact, most of them never again reach the heights of their initial stardom. Bobby Sherman, Fabian, and Davy Jones were just a few who suffered that fate. Frank Sinatra stands out as a teen idol who came back bigger than ever. The bobby-soxers delight of the early 1940s, Sinatra was miscast in a few Hollywood movies, only one of which, *On The Town*, was well received, (and that was mostly due to Gene Kelly, not Sinatra). He had pretty much been a forgotten figure until he agreed to take a small part in another movie for a measly $8,000. But his acting in *From Here To Eternity* won him an Academy Award and millions of new admirers who saw him as an actor, not a teen idol. He had waited a long time to be resurrected in the business, and he was one of the lucky ones.

Among the more recent teen casualties were David and Shaun Cassidy. David's five years on "The Partridge Family" earned him millions of dollars, gold records, screaming fans on his concert tours, and, after the show was cancelled, an empty feeling where his career had been. Ironically, David had debuted in television as a serious actor, winning kudos for his sensitive performances in dramas such as "Marcus Welby M.D." He had been warned about what could happen to his serious career, which had included a stint on Broadway in a musical, if he played a teenage singer on a TV program. But his stepmother, Shirley Jones, was the star name on "Partridge," and she recommended him. The steady money sounded great, so he agreed.

Long after the series had disappeared (except in syndication), David was still battling his teen image and trying to get back to the serious stage of his career. No matter what he did after "Partridge," reviewers always wrote about him as if he were still a lightweight in that series. All his previous acting raves were forgotten; only the teen label remained.

His half-brother Shaun, who had starred even more briefly in "The Hardy Boys Mysteries," suffered a similar fate. He, too, had been lured by the easy money, the chance to be a singing star, but even though he got rich, his career was left in shambles. The story was a familiar one, but not one likely to stop other hopefuls from following that path.

David Cassidy hoped that the 1980s would be the time when he could upgrade his image. When Broadway producers offered him the lead in the musical that would preview in Los Angeles, travel across America, and open in New York on Broadway in early 1982, he eagerly accepted. (Everyone in Hollywood is in awe of the legitimate theater and stars who can hold a live audience for eight performances a week.)

The musical was a revival of *Little Johnny Jones*, and it had been in trouble from the start, even though it was written by the immortal George M. Cohan and had two all-time hit numbers: "Give My Regards To Broadway" and "Yankee Doodle Dandy," (both of them songs that were sung to perfection by James Cagney when he won his Oscar for portraying superpatriot Cohan on film). The show's theme of good triumphing over evil was definitely dated. But with Reagan in the White House, and the country swerving to conservatism, the time seemed ripe for a warm-hearted, bubbly, old-fashioned musical about virtue.

When *Little Johnny Jones* debuted in Los Angeles, both the play and David Cassidy were panned. The play focused on the fortunes of an American jockey who goes to England to ride in the English Derby. When his horse loses, he is accused of throwing the race for a bookie who has been openly trying to get him to do just that. In the end, of course, Johnny Jones proves himself by winning another big race and winds up with the girl. Some of the reviews were ego shattering, but the show went on the road as planned after the L.A. date. The company hoped to smooth out the rough edges before getting to Broadway.

Nothing helped, however, and in Dallas, Cassidy dropped out. The show closed down temporarily while a new young leading man was sought, preferably someone like Cassidy with box office power among the audience.

That brought the producers to Donny Osmond. It did not take much coaxing to get Donny to agree. "I fell in love with the music because it is what I am, a true-blue American," he said. Donny knew he was facing the biggest challenge of his life. This was a big production with lots of singing and dancing, and a script with lines that had to be learned. Besides, when the shows are on the road, the cast often works around the clock, getting ready for the big day when they open on Broadway to the most important critics in the business. But Donny was willing to take the leap. It is possible his producers had doubts about his stamina and ability to make the quick changes that Broadway shows make before opening, but Donny rapidly proved himself and gained everyone's confidence. His aptitude for the stage and his commitment amazed even the veterans in the cast.

Few knew the havoc the show made of his personal life. The rehearsal hours were long and difficult, the performances exhausting, (especially for a novice), and he was in nearly every scene. Often he did not get back to Debbie and the boys until after midnight. None of the other Osmonds had ever worked this way before. The family-first dictum was taking a back seat to Donny's work, but Debbie gave her approval and rearranged the boys' schedule so that they could get some time with their daddy every day. No matter what time Donny dragged in, Debbie had the boys up and waiting. Then it was a quick romp with them and, if he hadn't dropped off to sleep in the middle, a quick bite and a few words with Debbie before he fell into bed. He was asleep before his head hit the pillow.

Why was Donny driving himself so hard? Certainly, even though the family entertainment center was in a state of flux, the Osmonds were in no danger of going broke. Besides, Donny was making far less in the show than he could have made from a concert tour or TV specials. But he was twenty-four-years old and very tired of being looked at as if he were still a sixteen-year-old warbling "Puppy Love."

And he was tired of the jokes about him and his family. If he could successfully carry a Broadway show, the jokes would stop and he might finally get some respect.

"I'm trying my darndest to prove to people that, yeah, I may have that wholesome image, but I'm very real," he admitted. "I've worked very hard, from rock bottom, to gain what I have. It wasn't handed to me on a silver platter."

The complaints got attention because people were not used to hearing an Osmond complain, to let out his pain. Donny seemed almost relieved to say, "Because I don't take drugs or drink I'm considered a square. People made fun of my smile. I get tired of that. I'm not a goody-goody."

Wherever the show traveled, Donny had the same problem. His image preceeded him, and he had to work twice as hard as the rest of the cast to prove his worth. But at least he was making an honest appraisal of the situation, not turning away as if it did not exist. And all of it centered on his need to be accepted as a mature performer. To another reporter he said, "I'm not a fake, I'm not a hypocrite. I don't have to smile when I don't want to. It drives me crazy sometimes when people think, 'oh, he's not real,' I am a real person. . . . I've got problems just like everybody, except I've got more because people call me 'plastic.'"

Still, whenever the cameras turned his way, Donny met them with a flash of teeth and that familiar Osmond grin. Old habits die hard.

By the time the show reached Washington, D.C., the reviews had gotten fairly good, raising everyone's hopes. What they forgot was that Washington was more apt to fall for the charm of *Little Johnny Jones'* apple-pie-and-mom formula than sophisticated and somewhat jaded New York. By now, though, Donny had dazzled the cast and crew with his energy. No one worked harder, no one put in longer hours. Broadway shows often became little families. Most of the people have left their loved ones behind because it is too expensive to travel with them. But even though Donny went home every night to Debbie and the boys, he built up a genuine rapport with his travel mates.

Meanwhile, back in Utah, Marie and the rest of the clan missed Donny as they hosted one of his favorite events. For several years they had run a skiing tournament close to Provo to raise funds for the U.S. Ski Team. Most of Hollywood turned out, just as they do at Clint Eastwood's or Alan King's tennis benefits and John Denver's skiing event in Colorado. Stars love to compete, and Marie, Alan, Wayne, Merrill, Jay, and even Jimmy, welcomed Connie Stevens, Randi Oakes, Paul Williams, Hal Linden, and a host of other TV stars to the weekend fund raiser. As usual, it was a big success, and the money raised will go a long way to getting the American ski team to the Olympics in 1984. Donny, who is an outstanding athlete, really hated missing it and sent his regrets, but he was completely wrapped up in *Little Johnny Jones*. Besides, he would soon be seeing the family.

The show pulled into New York, where rehearsals continued, in December. Donny and Debbie rented a lovely house across the river in Englewood, New Jersey, for what they hoped would be a lengthy stay. They opted for New Jersey, even though it was a longer commute for Donny, because they wanted Donny Jr. to have some space and a yard to play in. Debbie immediately fit into the suburban scene, and she spent her afternoons discovering all the discount stores.

Though the musical was getting cheers in preview performances, there was still something missing. Broadway shows often turn into battlegrounds as stars, producers, directors, and writers get worn down by the relentless schedule. *Little Johnny Jones* was no exception. Before its official New York opening, the director quit, demanding that his name be kept off the opening night programs and any future credit lists. Broadway gossips were quick to fill the public in on the problems. But Donny's name was never associated with the feuds or spats. His initiation into the Broadway elite was nearly complete.

There was one additional complication in Donny's life. Before embarking on his theater career, he had signed a multi-year contract with CBS to host the network's annual New Year's Eve Gala. Donny was trying to fill a big pair of shoes by taking over the spot that for decades had belonged to just one man, Guy Lombardo. As long as anyone could remember, Lombardo had been Mr. New Year's Eve, with America dancing to the sweet beat of his Royal Canadians on that grand evening. When he died, he left a void no one had been able to fill.

CBS believed Donny had the perfect assets to be the new emcee. He was young, well-known, and had an image that appealed to older folks. He was, after all, a key member of America's First Family of Song, and they hoped he could build up his own traditional following for the night. They dubbed him "Mr. Midnight," and from the stage at the Waldorf Astoria where he entertained the hundreds of couples paying hundreds of dollars for the evening, he introduced a lineup of rock and rhythm 'n' blues stars from around the country.

He had the right exuberance for the evening and seemed to enjoy himself as much as the audience. It was great exposure for the young entertainer, but it also meant double duty, trying to fit rehearsals in around his Broadway show. Somehow he managed, without one yawn, to bring the night to a successful conclusion.

The Broadway company was experienced enough to recognize that they were in trouble. But Donny's fans from all over the East Coast were flocking to the Alvin theater to see their idol in person. And they were ordering tickets for beyond opening night, a good sign.

Although he was exhausted from putting the show together, Donny, in typical Osmond fashion, hid that from fans who waited patiently for him to enter or leave the theater. The gracious star signed thousands of autographs and invited many of his fans backstage to visit after the performance, which meant he got home even later than usual. But the fans responded to his stage character enthusiastically, as did the preview audiences that came more for the Cohan music than for Donny. His plan was working, and it was clear that theater-goers took him seriously as a Broadway song-and-dance man. His ingratiating personality and candid honesty about his past also won him fans among the hard-to-please press. Donny was playing down his religion in interviews, although there were some principles still so deeply ingrained in him that he could not lightly dismiss one moment in the musical.

To most people Donny looked funny when he admitted that the kissing scene in the musical had given him some uneasy moments. In an age when performers think nothing of shedding all their clothes and parading around the stage naked, Donny's agony over a harmless kiss was amusing. Donny certainly had kissed women other than his wife, but it went against his beliefs to kiss one in public now that he was a married man. Ever since he had decided to move into acting, Donny feared this moment.

He admitted that he and Debbie "talked about it for years. I said, 'Honey, someday it's gonna happen,' and she accepts it very well. It's got to be hard, though, to sit out there and watch your husband kiss another woman."

Finally, opening night arrived. All the Osmonds were there to give Donny their support and to cheer in the audience. To their ears, there were lots of other laughs and applause that night in the theater. They believed the audience was having a grand time, right from the moment the audience was asked to stand while the National Anthem was played and a spotlight beamed down on an American flag in a nearby box, through the overture and up to Donny's rousing rendition of "Yankee Doodle Dandy."

When the curtain came down, the Osmonds rushed backstage to congratulate him. Then they were off to a nearby steak restaurant to await the reviews. Olive, George, and Marie raved about the musical and Broadway's newest star. Unfortunately, the Osmonds were naive about Broadway. The fact that audiences cheer on opening night makes little difference to a show's success or failure. That rests on the few remaining theater reviewers.

Little Johnny Jones, to the Osmonds' dismay, was shot down. The New York *Daily News'* Douglas Watt was kinder to the show and Donny than some. The influential reviewer reported that "Osmond's creamy good looks and toothpaste grin are familiar to most of America, and so I suppose, though I never caught him on the tube, is his engaging way with a song-and-dance number. But whereas

Cohan . . . is a feisty sort, Osmond is a colorless performer, however likeable."

That was the general tone of Donny's personal reviews. Likeable but lacking the stage presence that separate Broadway stars from television personalities. As for the show itself, Watt shrugged: "It's a nice try, but in a season notorious for its dearth of satisfactory new musicals, *Little Johnny Jones* is as stimulating as a package of sliced white bread."

Sometimes a show can succeed, even after terrible reviews, on the strength of the star's name. Undoubtedly that was in the back of the producers' minds when they hired teen idols for the lead. But, while Donny's name had sold a few thousand tickets, that was not nearly good enough to keep such an expensive production running. The Osmonds were stunned when, at the opening night party, the producers posted the closing night notice. There would be no more performances.

Donny was very upset. Several hundred tickets were sold for the next day's show, and as an Osmond, he felt an obligation to honor the ticket holder's faith in him. But he learned the fans would have to be content with getting their money back because it was just too expensive to mount the show and the producers were not about to throw good money after bad.

On that sad note, Donny and Debbie gave up their house and went home to Utah. The experience had whet his appetite for more stage work, and he promised that the next time he would come back to Broadway in a dramatic play.

But, when the end of the year rolled around and the reviewers began compiling their best-and-worst-ten lists of the season past, *Little Johnny Jones* made most of the worst Broadway shows lists. Doubtless, no one could have saved such a dated musical, not while theater-goers were making *Evita* and *A Chorus Line* standing-room-only performances.

8

A Secret Love

Marie was the Osmond who took the closing of *Little Johnny Jones* harder than anyone, even Donny. As the one closest to her brother, she knew best how much time and effort he had poured into the show and how much he had wanted to demonstrate that he was more than just another aging teen idol. It was true that they both had no regrets about growing up in show business, but now it was all they knew, and the Osmond drive for success was as strong within them as ever.

Besides, Marie would miss Donny when he returned to Utah because she was staying on. Marie had been in New York for several weeks and was planning a long stay, but it was not a publicized visit. When her TV movie, *Side By Side*, was about to be aired, she made the usual round of talk shows promoting the film. And there were surprised faces when Marie revealed that she had left Provo for New York. When asked why she was making such a drastic move, Marie explained that it was time she took acting seriously. So she had enrolled in the Actors Studio in order to pursue her goal.

The Studio numbers among its illustrious alumni Marlon Brando, James Dean, Ellen Burstyn, Al Pacino, Robert DeNiro, and a slew of other famous Hollywood stars. It is the most respected acting school in the country, and its reputation is founded on good teaching. It is mainly a workshop school where students are constantly called on to work out scenes, which are then carefully analyzed. Everyone within the Studio walls is very serious about the art of acting, and the frivolous are turned away, although anyone wishing to push her creativity to new heights is welcome. The school selects pupils based on their potential; it does not care what prior image that person brings along.

Other young performers had entered the Studio under circumstances similar to Marie's, who now accepted that she needed a change of image before her acting would be taken seriously. The same had been true of Sally Field. She had played Gidget and the Flying Nun for so many years that, eventually, those were the only kind of parts she was offered. But Sally outgrew those sweet, teenage roles and would have been long forgotten if not for the Actors Studio. Instead, she became one of the truly dedicated actresses, turning down TV series and movies while using up all her energies in workshop productions to shape a whole new acting style. Ultimately, it paid off for her, although it took some three years of her life. But without that strong sense of purpose, she never would have won awards for *Sybil* and *Norma Rae*, roles that opened up new creative opportunities for her.

Marie was eager for the same success, but there was another, and for her, far more important motive behind her extended stay. Marie had been dating a certain young athlete and his career had brought him east. But to keep the tabloids from discovering this secret love, Marie was avoiding any dates with him where they might be spotted and photographed.

There had been many handsome men in her life since her split from Jeff Crayton, from Dirk Benedict and Andy Gibb to the young blond star of "The Dukes of Hazzard," John Schneider. (Much had been made of their dates because they made such an adorable couple with their contrasting blond and brunette heads.) Marie did not deny that she was fond of John, but it never got beyond that stage. They were just good friends. Besides, as long as she showed up at show-business events with famous escorts, it drew attention from the man she was really falling for, Steve Craig.

Craig was a handsome, six-feet-three-inch star on the Brigham Young University basketball team when Marie had met him. A friend of Jay's, Steve and Marie kept bumping into each other and learned they had a lot in common. Best of all, Steve was not just a jock; he was bright and articulate. Marie was like all young girls, of course; she preferred attractive men, but looks weren't everything. "Physical attraction is very important," she said, "But I don't care if someone turns me on—if I can't talk to him, forget it."

Steve was easy to talk to, and yet, he was not in awe of her the way Crayton had been, probably because Steve was used to being around movie stars and their kids. He was from Los Angeles and had graduated from Beverly Hills High, which is filled with the children of famous stars; his dad was an athletic coach at the school. So he grew up surrounded by the biggest names in show business.

Marie and Steve dated often, but usually in a group of friends, so nobody could get nosy about the handsome guy with her. She had been stung too often by seeing her name linked with a new date and headlines about their wedding day. Marie was not going to have Steve embarrassed, nor was she ready to make a big decision as she still smarted from the Crayton affair. The couple kept it casual, but their friends recognized all the signs.

When they first met, Steve was still playing for BYU. Marie was often on the campus, taking courses and hanging out with her pals. Her brothers were all sports buffs, so it was natural that she show up at basketball games to cheer—for Steve, of course. "The first time I saw him on the basketball court," Marie later said, "I thought he had cute legs." The rest of him wasn't bad either. He was ruggedly built and had blond hair and green eyes; Marie felt herself falling in love.

But Marie was still too close to her first engagement to rush things. Mutual friends encouraged the twosome. In spite of her successful career, close chums could not help but notice a certain sadness about Marie. Her inclinations were more toward domestic skills than her career, and obviously she was anxious to find a husband and build her own home. After she gave Jeff back his ring, she rather wistfully admitted that while her room in her parents house was very pleasant and decorated to her own taste, what she really wanted was a home of her own and babies.

Children were especially important to Marie. All of her married brothers had families, and she envied their closeness. Without children of her own, she had to settle for the loving relationships with her nieces and nephews.

In the Mormon church, when a child reaches its eighth year, it is baptized formally into the church. Every Osmond child knows that on that special day there is an extra treat in store, because Marie initiated a lovely tradition with her nieces and nephews. After their baptism, each child gets to spend the afternoon alone with Marie, doing whatever they want. She takes the honored guest shopping or to a movie and then out for dinner, which makes the youngster feel very grownup and very close to Aunt Marie.

Around her family, Marie has always been domestic. Since she was thirteen, Marie has single-handedly prepared the Osmonds' Thanksgiving dinner. Considering the ever-growing number of Osmonds, that is almost a miraculous feat, but she does it as a personal way of saying thank you to Olive and the rest of the family.

Things like this make Marie the kind of girl Steve had been searching for; he certainly did not want a career woman, although if continuing her career on a part-time basis made Marie happy, he could accept it. But he wanted a full-time mother for his family. That suited Marie completely.

Marie never failed to discuss her love life with Olive, and when she began talking about Steve all the time, Mrs. Osmond saw what was coming. Fortunately, the family heartily approved of Steve. Whereas Jeff had been a struggling actor-singer when engaged to Marie, Steve was talented in his own field and would not have to compete with her family. It seems the Osmonds had cooled on Jeff after his father told a reporter that he would not be surprised to see

Jeff onstage with his inlaws after the wedding. Osmond wives have never been allowed in the act, so it did not seem wise to make an exception for anyone Marie might marry. They did not have to worry about Steve.

The Craigs were very much like the Osmonds, except for a neat reverse; Steve had five sisters and only one brother. Marie liked the idea of getting five new sisters instantly. And the Craigs were devout Mormons, which is what brought Steve to BYU.

At twenty-five, he was older than most of the students and the basketball players, but he had left BYU to serve his two years with the Mormon mission in El Salvador. He had returned to BYU and was completing his degree in public relations. He had everything any family could want for their daughter—good looks, brains, and a strong inner faith.

Just as Marie wanted to become an actress, so too did Steve have his dreams. Ever since he was a boy, he had wanted to be a professional athlete. His basketball prowess had brought him national fame, and when he completed his final year of college eligibility, he got his wish. He was a fifth-round draft choice of the Philadelphia 76ers of the National Basketball Association.

There are only twelve men on a pro basketball team, however, and hundreds of talented newcomers are drafted every year, even though only two or three rookies actually make each team in any given year. With such odds, Steve was disappointed but not really surprised when he failed to gain a spot on the 76ers. He was encouraged when they urged him to play for one of their farm clubs, also in Pennsylvania, even though it meant a separation from Marie.

But Marie was not about to let Steve get away, which is why she came to New York. There was no way she could show up in a small Pennsylvania town without drawing attention to herself, and the last thing Steve needed was publicity about his love life when he was fighting to make the pros. For the next few months their relationship was sustained more via telephone than actual dates, but that did not change the way they felt about each other.

But before Steve could say much, Marie was off again

with her family, this time to Bermuda. While she was away, she and Steve burned up the phone wires. As soon as she returned, he joined her in Utah and popped the question. Marie did not hesitate and practically said yes before he asked. The happy couple were not overly eager to set their wedding date, but there were forces at play behind the scenes that speeded up their decision.

Marie's parents had been born in difficult times; they had survived a depression, fallen in love and married while a war was raging, and raised a large family. During all of that, they had considerations larger than their own personal desires to worry about. But with their children grown and on their own, and with their financial position secure, George and Olive felt the call to at last fulfill their Mormon obligation as missionaries. They informed their family that they would be leaving shortly for the mission based in Hawaii, and since they could not interrupt the two years for any personal business, Marie would have to get married before they left. Steve and Marie announced their engagement in May and set the wedding day for June 26, so her parents could be there to share her joy.

Right after the engagement news, Marie had to sail off to Monte Carlo for a month-long "Love Boat" location shoot. By now, she was used to her career interfering with her personal life, but she expected that to end once she was Mrs. Steve Craig.

But at least Steve was not the type to be found sitting home and pining; he was just as involved with his own career. Basketball players live much the way the Osmonds do, out of suitcases. Schedules are tough and the farm teams make most of their jumps between towns by bus, not first-class planes. The players grab hamburgers along the way and watch the standings of their parent clubs with great interest. The only way a player moves up to the big leagues is if one of the regulars gets hurt and his own stats are good enough to get him the call. It doesn't happen very often, and the fact that there are any number of former big leaguers also in the talent pool who usually get the first call for openings makes it that much tougher. It's that old vicious circle of everyone wanting experienced players, but how do you get the experience if nobody ever calls you up to play.

Steve often was tired from his grueling schedule, but he was not a complainer. Anything worth having, he knew, must be hard won. And he had the drive and ambition to go for his big goal, no matter how tough the odds. That is what drew Marie to him in the first place, that core of deep purpose that seemed to guide him.

Once again they carried on their romance via telephone, just as Marie had to plan her wedding by long distance. Fortunately with the aid of her family and friends, by the time she arrived home, just two days before the ceremony, the plans were in place.

This time, the lovely young woman had no doubts. She could hardly wait to walk into the Temple to join Steve in holy wedlock. And there was no question but that she was going to become simply "Mrs. Craig." Many professional women these days either retain their maiden names after marrying or insist on hyphenating theirs with their husband's name. But Marie and Steve were too tradition-bound for such liberated notions. For career purposes, she would remain Marie Osmond, simply because it would be too cumbersome to alter that. (In the future, it is possible that she will introduce herself even in movies and TV as Marie Craig; it is just a matter of letting people get used to the new name.) In Provo, however, she planned to use her husband's name. She had waited too long for this moment to cheat herself of that privilege. Besides, Steve wanted it that way.

9

Marie's Wedding Day

Marie's life had been in turmoil since Steve's proposal. Usually she relaxed and had a grand time with the cast and crew whenever she did "Love Boat." The Saturday night ABC series had been popular for years because it played up to every woman's fantasies about love and romance. A man and woman met, fell madly in love, but couldn't marry because of any number of sad or funny complications. In the end, every week, however, there were three happy marriages. Women were sweeping romance back into everyday life in the 1980s, not only with shows like the "Love Boat" but with romantic novels. Even teenagers had fallen under the spell of pure, chaste love.

But all the time she was filming in Monte Carlo, where the cast chanced to meet the royal family just weeks before the tragic death of Princess Grace, all Marie could think about was the smell of orange blossoms and her wedding day. It was a time when she should have been sharing intimate confidences with her friends and going to parties and showers. Instead, as usual, she was toiling away in some far corner of the world when she wanted to be back home, doing the normal little tasks brides-to-be take for granted. But there was no way she could suddenly pull out of the show. The vignettes were written weeks in advance, and the cast was chosen very carefully so that the romances could be built around particular personalities. In a way, though, it must have been a relief to be away from all the activity, which can wear a girl down.

She realized that it was not an easy time for Steve either. The Philadelphia team could not find a place for him, so he was cut from the farm club. Now, besides waiting for his wedding day, Steve was worried about ever making it to the pros. Marie understood what it was like to have a dream, to yearn for a spot many seek but few can reach. Her family had been very lucky; they had achieved their fame. She did not want Steve frustrated by losing his. When they spoke, she was loving and supportive, standing by her man as if she were already his wife.

Most brides awaiting their wedding day find that time sometimes seems to just stand still and other days seems to fly by as if someone just ripped the page off the calander. Marie was luckier than most; she was caught up in a job that required all of her concentration. And, having filmed other segments over the years, she had friends among the "Love Boat" regulars to share her joy as the big day approached. June 26 would be the culmination of all her most secret desires. Marie had been planning for this, after all, since she was seven years old. Her hope chest was filled with wonderful and precious objects from around the world, each one bringing back a memory of where and when it was purchased. At last, she could appreciate the time and patience her mother had poured into that collection.

Finally, she was back home in Provo, with just two days to attend to the final details. Her mother and friends had done a wonderful job preparing the wedding and reception.

At last, on the eve of her wedding day, Marie and the wedding party drove the forty-five miles to Salt Lake City where, of course, she and Steve would be joined in the great Temple. They were staying overnight at the Hotel Utah because the proceedings were scheduled to start early in the morning.

Marie awoke early on her wedding day. If she had been allowed to order the weather for this sacred ceremony, she could not have done better than the clear blue skies and warm sunshine she found outside her window. Surely that was a good omen of the perfect life she and Steve had ahead of them. The Greeks believe it is good luck when it rains on the wedding day, but most women dream of sunshine and cloudless skies, because rain can make you sad while sunshine makes you glad.

There was much bustling about as Marie slipped into her exquisite bridal gown. She had chosen a friend in Hollywood, costume designer Ret Turner, to help her design her dream gown. Something about bridal gowns make women feel fragile and delicate, and they want their gowns to capture those impressions. Marie's gown looked as if it had just materialized out of a fairytale where it had been worn by a princess who lived happily ever after. It was pure white silk taffeta covered with lace and tiny seed pearls. Underneath was a silk organza petticoat. But the crowning glory of the storybook gown was its sixteen-foot-long train. Several attendants would be required to get it into the church. In some ways it resembled the train that Princess Diana wore when she married Charles, the Prince of Wales. And, considering the guest list, Marie's wedding was the closest anyone has come to that widely-acclaimed extravaganza. There was one difference, however: the future King and Queen of England had been televised taking their vows. That was fine for the Anglican church, but the Mormons considered marriage too sacred to allow outsiders to view the ceremony.

It was still early morning, long before most of the city had awakened that June 26, when Marie and her wedding party were ready to leave for the Temple. Warm, considerate, and loving Marie had wanted to spread her joy that day like a mantle over everyone. Her attendants were to be Steve's five sisters, a few nieces, and two friends. Her eight brothers and Steve's one would also be involved in the wedding.

Marie and the others quietly slipped out of the hotel and entered the ninety-year-old Temple, the most famous of all the Mormon shrines. If she had a moment's doubt, she never showed it. Inside, Steve, looking elegant in a white dinner jacket that set off his sparkly green eyes, was waiting.

Mormons don't go in for long, complicated ceremonies. The young couple exchanged the vows their brethren have been saying for centuries, promising to love one another "for time and all eternity." They also exchanged simple gold wedding bands, and by the power vested in Paul Dunn, the church elder and long-time friend the Osmonds had asked to perform the ceremony, Marie and Steve were joined in holy matrimony forever.

The actual marriage rite may be brief in the Mormon religion, but the wedding celebration goes on far into the night. After the vows, the newlyweds and the rest of their entourage were led through a private passageway to the Lion House. This is a reception area that was once owned by Brigham Young himself. There they enjoyed a leisurely wedding breakfast.

As they were leaving to return to the hotel, one of Marie's nieces noticed that the lovely train to her gown had gotten dirty. Marie laughed delightedly and told the little girl, "That's okay, I'm only going to do this once."

The rest of the day was spent in quiet conversation with their families and selected close friends. So much must have been whirling through Marie's mind at that moment. Her fondest dream had just been realized and yet there was probably a degree of sadness, too. Because, very soon, her closest confidante would be leaving, just when there would be so much to tell and to ask. Once Olive and George were settled in the Hawaii mission, contact would be severely limited, but Marie could not say anything; she knew what this commitment meant to them.

But for the rest of that day, there was only the great joy and jubilation that follows marriage. The day passed swiftly and as evening fell, guests began arriving for the grand reception.

Four thousand people had been invited, among them their beloved mentor, Andy Williams. The ballroom was fragrant with thousands of fresh white roses that covered the walls. The bridesmaids looked especially elegant in their multicolored gowns, ranging from white to blue, pink, peach, yellow, and green.

Marie and Steve tried to get around and personally greet each guest and thank them for coming. As they did so, the guests presented them with their wedding gifts while dining on lobster and shrimp, washed down with the Osmonds favorite beverage—Hawaiian Punch.

From the glow on Marie's cheeks, it was apparent that she was deeply in love and very happy. But if anyone had doubts, she was heard to exclaim, "I'll never find anyone I love more than Steve."

The newlyweds held hands and did their best to be good hosts. Finally, the wedding cake was brought out and the guests oohed and aahed over what was truly an overwhelming concoction. It was a carrot cake, well over five feet high, and the icing was covered with handmade sugar roses, hundreds of them. The cake was a masterpiece that had taken three weeks to bake and assemble. There were enough pieces for everyone and many of those pieces must have wound up under single girls' pillows, something to dream on and hope that one day they would find a Steve Craig of their own. The party went splendidly with all the guests wishing Steve and Marie a long and happy life.

The guests were still partying when Steve and Marie departed. Outside was a Cadillac limousine to take them on their three-day honeymoon. Neither would reveal where they were going. Marie wanted to keep it as their private retreat, a place they could return to over the years to recapture their honeymoon spirit. "I have never thought anything could be so wonderful and so fulfilling," Marie sighed just after returning from the honeymoon.

If those three days were any indication, Marie believed that she and Steve could have as happy and lasting a relationship as her own parents, who, she said, were still close and loving after thirty-seven years and left each other love notes on their pillows. They were still frisky enough for water fights, too, which is what Marie looked forward to in years to come.

Most new couples are madly in love when they marry. But psychologists point out that the passions that bring people together naturally wane as couples settle into marriage. And then they need good communication and honesty as well as love to survive. The Craigs were well versed in this subject and had vowed that there would be no secrets between them.

The only problem that might mar their happiness was the state of Marie's health. Once again, between the wedding and her career, she had been very close to illness. She needed to slow down, but that was not possible, at least not for the next few weeks, as once again she would be hitting the singing trail. Meanwhile, Steve would be living in their Provo home while he continued at the university. He still had a few credits to finish to earn his degree in public relations. He wanted his degree, and besides, it gave him something constructive to do while Marie was on tour.

The parting was not without its heartache, though, since they had had so little time to actually be together. Both were aware that there would be some hard work ahead as they tried to blend their two life styles into one. And as long as Marie had to work, that would be difficult. But Steve was mature enough to accept being married to a professional woman.

Marie was the one who was questioning pursuing her career. Ever since she had been a tiny child and intent on one day marrying a handsome husband, she had vowed that she would be content as a housewife. Now and again she might cut some records, but Marie quite frankly was tired of the tours and eager to have a life of her own apart from the family act. Perhaps now that she was no longer alone, but had Steve in her corner, she could follow her own instincts, which said she wanted to be homebound for a while and to start her family. Traveling was fine for her brothers; they were embarking on a new phase of their career and needed the exposure. But she was newly married and had been home so little, it was remarkable she could remember her own address.

10

Still Singing After All These Years

Travel for the Osmonds was just an accepted part of their existence. So Marie thought nothing of making a tour of more than thirty cities shortly after becoming Mrs. Craig. Most nights the Osmond Brothers opened the show with their new country hits, but most of the booking agents who hired the Osmonds did so for Donny and, especially, Marie. They were the stars that brought people into the hall. Marie had blossomed into the most versatile of the singers, always giving the fans an inspiring show. Marie's overpowering energy seemed to sweep through the crowds.

But a person can push the human body just so far before it rebels. The tour exhausted the newlywed; getting back to Steve was a welcome relief. She knew she loved this tall, strong, wonderful guy on their wedding day, but it was not until she came home from a tour that she fully appreciated what he brought into her life. Theirs was truly a marriage of equals. Rather than expecting Marie to turn into the little housefrau when she came off her tour, he took care of her, especially after she gave him the happy news: she was pregnant.

Now they had a new reason to decorate their rambling, five-bedroom home in Provo. Her parents had found it in the '70s and bought it for themselves, but as they were going to Hawaii for an extended stay, the house made a wonderful present for Steve and Marie. Once the home of Rose Marie Reid, the famous swimsuit designer and manufacturer, it was very secluded, surrounded by trees and land, a perfect spot for the honeymooners. Together they worked side by side to remodel it before the baby came. They wanted to modernize it, to paint one of the bedrooms in bright pastels for the baby, since psychologists say that children respond to cheery colors, which help them to develop faster.

Once Marie told Steve about her condition, however, he insisted she leave the heavy remodeling work to him. Although they had been married just a couple of months before Marie got pregnant, neither of them regretted starting their family so soon. Their love was so strong that they did not need to work at their relationship before adding another member of the family. They were totally compatible, and Marie had trouble containing her joy, so excited was she about finally having a baby all her own.

Marie should have sailed right through the pregnancy, but, although she had always promised she would retire from singing when she was married and starting a family, the rest of the Osmonds wanted her on yet another tour they had booked. Marie's continued touring made her the object of much speculation, with the consensus holding that the family was forcing her to go out on the road with them because she was the moneymaker, and the family fortune was crumbling. Some headlines charged the Osmonds with using poor Marie as their empire came apart at the seams and they stood on the edge of bankruptcy.

All doubters had to do, insiders said, was to watch Marie push herself to perform. With her history of illness coupled with the normal pressures of pregnancy, they concluded that the family was putting its greed above Marie's safety and need. And again, they called the entertainment center a "white elephant."

Such vicious talk angered the Osmonds, who rarely express strong negative emotion. They could not deny, however, that the entertainment center in Orem that had been opened with such high expectations was a steady drain on their finances. Since "The Donny and Marie Show" had been canceled, they had not been able to lure any other weekly show to the wilds of Utah. They were able to rent it out to the occasional cable or syndicated show, but not often enough to make the center pay. As for selling their distribution arm, that was a wise course after their grandiose plans to produce several movies a year had been put on the back burner after they were burned with their first two releases. But the recording studio was in constant use, mostly by the Osmonds, who were still putting albums together. However, they did so from desire, not need. The simple truth is that the Osmonds are very wealthy.

Very quietly over the years, the Osmonds, under George's level-headed supervision, had diversified into many non-entertainment areas. Ever since they were married, the elder Osmonds had been buying up property in Utah, and once the boys made it, and made California their base, the Osmonds expanded their purchases to properties on the West Coast. Both had turned into boom areas. The family had heavy investments in shopping malls, a cattle ranch, apartment houses, and some of the most fertile farmland around. With all of this, if they ever wanted to retire, they would never have money worries. Just one of their farms, the Brenda Mesa Farms nestled in California's San Joaquin Valley, is one of the largest agricultural complexes in America. It supplies most of the almonds and pistachios that are popular around the world. Under the farm's "Bountiful" label, Brenda Mesa packages and distributes many other farm products. It is a highly profitable operation.

In fact, the Osmonds, who had earned an estimated $10 million per year at the height of their popularity, are regarded as one of the wealthiest families in the business, making the headlines about financial ruin ridiculous. If necessary, the family could have shut down the entertainment complex entirely, cut their losses, and continued to live in fine fashion. But they are fighters, and they are confident that, as has happened in the past, tastes will come full circle and their entertaining style will be popular once more, leading to another TV series and, they hope, movies.

If the Osmonds take their current successful comeback as any guide, it seems to lend credence to their argument. Not only have they been gaining impressive sales with their country song style and winning awards, but there is great interest in the syndicated radio show they have put together. The show is expected to make Billy Bob's club in Fort Worth, Texas, as popular as John Travolta's *Urban Cowboy* made Gilley's, the huge club owned by country-western singer Mickey Gilley. What with guests like Merle Haggard, Tammy Wynette, and Waylon Jennings, how can it miss?

Although having Marie along to ensure crowds at country fairs and country festivals, the fact that the Osmond Brothers have placed their new songs near the top of the country charts is enough to get them decent bookings. But Marie has a way of bringing a spritely quality to their act that keeps the fans in a good mood.

No one, of course, forces Marie to go along, but she does feel an obligation to be with her family on tour. She has known no other life for twenty years and while there are times she wishes she were home, five minutes into her routine, she forgets her weariness. Watching the fans get into the spirit of her act makes her own face light up with joy.

But a baby makes new demands on any woman. The body can undergo dramatic changes in chemical balance, and pregnant women need more rest; they are carrying around a lot of excess weight and trying to eat enough to nourish two. Doctors also recommend staying off your feet to avoid varicose veins. At the best of times, Marie was fragile; her pregnancy had her whole family concerned.

Steve also was concerned when Marie joined her family for another hectic round of concerts. At first, it did not appear that she would have any difficulty; it was still early in her pregnancy and she did not show. But the travel and demanding work got to Marie. After one of their concerts down South, she told her brothers she could not continue; she was going home and did not expect to be back until the baby was born.

Alan and his brothers were supportive of Marie. But he realized that she would be missed; she was the irreplaceable one in the act. The tour continued, but some of the bounce was gone.

Meanwhile, Steve was getting some disappointing news of his own. Another professional basketball team had contacted him, and Steve tried out for the San Diego Clippers, only to get cut again. All was not lost, though, and he worked on getting in shape for another tryout. This time, Marie really hoped he would make the squad because it was practically in their backyard. And, indeed, Steve believed he had his best shot yet with the Utah Jazz because he had been a college star in the area and that can be an incentive for fans to come out and watch a home-town player.

When their careers did not get in the way, the couple continued decorating their house, but the repairs were so extensive, they had to move out for a few months. Their new temporary quarters were in their weekend home in Sundance; it was close enough to Provo to continue their renovations, but far enough away for Marie to take long walks, relax, and think about their future.

Marie was not totally preoccupied with domestic affairs. When Steve came home and told her he had made the Jazz, they celebrated. At last, he was making his boyhood dream a reality. A few days later, the joy turned to sadness when Steve broke his foot, which would keep him off the team and set his training program back at least a year. That might have upset another young man, but while they were unhappy about the turn of events, they believed that whatever happened, happened for the best. And behind every cloud was a silver lining; now Steve would be able to complete the house before the baby was born.

Steve's tough break did not keep Marie off the concert trail. There must have been doubts in the songstress' mind before tackling her new assignment. Besides, she had just filmed a Christmas special, "A Solid Gold Christmas," before hitting the road. This was a shorter tour, mainly in Arizona, Vegas, and Florida. She was not the kind of woman who considered herself a fragile flower, but the truth was that she had stretched her body to the limits.

In Florida she nearly collapsed and had to leave the

show. Tired and drawn, Marie flew home to Steve's loving arms. He indicated that this time, no matter what, she would not return to work. There were no objections from Marie. Instead, she said, "For the first time Steve and I will have all the time in the world to do things other couples like to do, like go to a movie or out to dinner." For Marie, a whole new world was opening, the world where normal married couples lived.

Steve, too, began looking in new directions. With his pro career postponed, he needed a job, and what he wanted was something to do with sports. He had been a successful player at Brigham Young University, so it was natural that he would turn to his coaches there for advice. Since he had been a star, the new players admired and respected him.

Steve is very bright and easy-going and kids respond well to him. When he asked the coaches for advice at his alma mater, he discovered that there was an opening right under his nose at the university. Not only would he be earning a salary, but it would help him snap back into shape quickly, too.

He became the junior varsity coach at the school and he really enjoyed working with the younger players. Steve was a natural with them, maybe because he had grown up with a coach for a dad. They learned a lot from him, especially as he stressed the fundamentals of the game. Coaches often become father figures to their charges, so Steve was also getting in some practice at a role he would soon be playing for real.

Marie began to experience the wonderful changes taking place in her body as the baby grew inside her. As happens in moments like this, she found a new maturity, saying, "I feel my life is moving through seasons." First she had been a child and now she was to be a mother. It was so much like the song that warns parents and children that, in what seems like a moment, the little ones turn around and are soon grown up and going out the door. The Mormons encouraged their families to continually leaf through their Books of Remembrance, to see the seasons of each person's life. Women seem more sensitive to these changes since they are the bearers of life.

The days passed pleasantly as Marie exercised regularly and worked in her garden. But, she truly is a creature of habit and she could not toss aside the work ethic she had carried for a lifetime. When she finally had the time to be just a wife and mother, Marie grew restless.

Marie was so much like her mother in this respect; neither has ever been able to endure idle hands. Again, like her mother, Marie loved to design clothes, a hobby that can be traced back to her childhood when she and Olive would discuss fabrics and patterns by the hour before making a choice. At the height of her television fame, Marie and Olive had actually designed their own line of clothes under the "Olive's Kids" label for Butterick Patterns. The clothes were the kind Marie wore, but they never really caught on with the kids, and when the show was dropped, so was the "Marie" line of fashions. However, she still believed that she had a knack for creating interesting and useful clothes.

A local Utah manufacturer also believed in Marie and signed her to design a clothing line for girls, along with a maternity wardrobe. Who was better qualified right then than Marie, who complained there were few good exercise clothes for the mother-to-be and promptly put a collection together. Best of all, the manufacturer was practically next door, so Marie had complete control over the finished product. And the clothes would be sold throughout Utah, where her name carried some weight.

Under her doctor's supervision, Marie was also exercising regularly. Even before she was pregnant, she had always done one hundred situps each morning, but with the baby, she wanted to do exercises that would help in the birthing process.

Fitness has become the national pastime, with joggers competing with cars for road space and bikers banging into each other on the highways. Exercise and health foods—honey instead of white sugar, bran, no red meat, and the like are major sources of conversation at parties—where Perrier has replaced champagne. Bookstores are filled with diagram-heavy texts all designed to make a shaplier, slimmer you.

Marie could not help but notice how popular these books were, especially when a top celebrity's name was attached. There was Richard Simmons, who parlayed a recurring role on a daytime soap into an exercise and life-style book and that into a best-selling record and, finally, his own television show. Jane Fonda was another surprising entry in the fitness field. She had begun with a fitness gym she developed in California for working women. Naturally, it had caught on with other stars and before long, Jane was opening up her fitness salons in other major cities. And it must follow as the night does the day that she do a book. *Jane Fonda's Workout Book* became the national number one bestseller and spawned a record and video cassette of the slim superstar at work keeping her body fit for all those wonderful roles she played.

Marie found a void in the bookshelves. She could not find a single helpful simple guide to exercise for pregnant women, or anything to help get women back in shape once the baby was born. So Marie was in her maternity clothes working out as she posed for the illustrations. All of these projects helped Marie stay busy until the little Craig arrived.

And on April 21, 1983, Marie gave birth to 7lb. 7 oz. Stephen James Craig. "This is the most incredible thing I've ever done," Marie exclaimed proudly from her hospital bed. But, she added, it was her mother, Olive, who was the most excited about the baby. Of course, George and Olive, who were still in Hawaii on their Mormon mission, were among the first to hear the good news. Naturally Marie was asked when the baby would join the Osmond act, especially since the new mother was embarking on yet another concert tour in July. Marie replied the baby would remain home with a nanny and Steve; she would not drag him around the world.

Ever since the Osmonds started marrying, there has been a question mark about their children: would they add the tiny tots to the act?—a sure-fire way to attract new fans. As of now, none has shown any inclination to expose their kids to the world they lived in, growing up in the limelight.

For her part, Marie is adamant about giving her children

a normal homelife. While she never expresses bitterness toward her parents, who took her away from Utah when she was only three, Marie has been very outspoken about the most commonplace moments she has missed in life. True, she has met royalty and toured world capitals, but she was eighteen before she went to her first dance, a prom for which she had an arranged date. Just watching the other kids at the dance left her feeling a bit empty inside. Steve came from a more normal background, but despite their differences, they shared similar views on raising their first child.

"Our parents taught us the value of hard work," she explained, "and that's what Steve and I are going to teach our children. I believe in discipline." The other Osmonds seem to be like-minded. Merrill introduced his son at an early age on a segment of Donny and Marie's show, and Donny brought his firstborn, Donald Clark Jr., on stage for his debut during one of the family's Christmas specials, but that is the sum total of their active participation in the family show.

The possibility exists that some of the children will arrive in the business on their own. It is only natural for a child to follow in his or her parents footsteps, but in this case, it will be the child's choice. Most of the Osmonds hold their own Family Night—but they have not turned it into a rehearsal hall—yet. None of them would trade places with the fans they've met from small towns, but, like the fans who fantasize about what it must be like to live the life of a star, so, too, must the Osmonds, now and again, ponder what it would be like to be just another Ogden family. They'll never know the answer, but it can be fun daydreaming about it.

Right before Marie's baby son was born, the family had more good news to celebrate. Their little brother Jimmy was coming home for good. In America, he was the forgotten Osmond as his career had led him to Japan where he was a major superstar, as big with Orientals as Donny had been at home.

The Japanese love children, and when Jimmy, at age three, was there with the Andy Williams show, his Vegas style with a song had captivated the audience. For many years, when he was not with the family in Vegas or some of their major play dates, he would fly back to Japan. When he was sixteen, his parents agreed to let him live there several months a year, and he had become a mini-mogul! He produced records in Tokyo, brought in concert acts, hosted his own TV series, and did a soft drink commercial that became an instant hit with his fans. In Japan, Jimmy was king.

"I love working over there," he said, "I even learned the language, at least enough to get me in trouble," he laughed. But, when he turned nineteen, Jimmy discovered how much he missed the familiar surroundings of America and his family. "What I want to do now is come back to my country and work here. Right now I'm studying acting in Los Angeles," he continued.

Jimmy is an ambitious Osmond and he wants to blend acting with singing for a well-rounded career. But his credentials from Japan didn't take him far in Des Moines, where he was unknown.

That changed, however, when he joined the cast of the NBC series "Fame" in 1982. The spin-off of the hit movie of that same name had never been a ratings hit, but NBC kept it around because it scored very high with the teenage audience, one of the most affluent and influential nowadays. As a retarded boy with an unusual gift for music that brings him to the High School of Performing Arts, which serves as the dramatic and musical backdrop for the series, Jimmy had his work cut out for him. The show has high standards for performers, but Jimmy sailed right through, and his role was expanded. For most young actors, this kind of role would be an ideal showcase. And so it was for Jimmy. The only drawback was the same one that hindered his sister's and brother Donny's careers: their strict moral code.

With movies mirroring the real world today, there are very few that could meet the restrictions Jimmy and his siblings place on acceptable roles. Anything suggestive is a no-no. Even the wonderfully warm-hearted and supremely successful *E.T.* used realistic, four-letter language in the young stars' dialogue, and one of the other main characters, the mother, was divorced!

But Jimmy does not mind being considered a goody-goody at this stage of his career. He candidly says that "some of the parts I've been offered I've had to turn down. Some of it is not morally for me: sex scenes and crazy things like that. I would never do that because that's just not me. As an actor, I'll deal with the real issues, but I don't think it's necessary to do things that I don't believe in, like sex scenes or profanity." Such impossibly high moral standards are more likely to lead to famine than fame when it comes to movie roles.

With Jimmy making news, there will be a replay of the Osmond headlines of the early '70s, when their religious laws made them objects of curiosity. Of course, Mormon doctrine is constantly changing, something that eludes many reporters.

The Osmonds, for example, tried to sidestep one of the major controversies of their early stardom days, when blacks were not permitted to hold the highest offices in the church. Whenever they were questioned on this subject, the Osmonds grew obviously embarrassed, murmuring that the church was constantly reexamining its policies. They never believed anyone inferior because of race, religion, color, or creed, but they were staunch defenders of the church and could not bring themselves to speak out against this practice.

Possibly because the Osmonds were considered goodwill ambassadors for Mormonism and yet refused to agree with the policy of racial inferiority, the elders met and reinterpreted the passages that had excluded blacks from full participation. It came too late to change the publicity the elder Osmonds were exposed to, but it saves Jimmy from similar embarrassment.

What the Osmonds can also point to with pride are recent studies based on several generations of research subjects that reveal Mormons commonly live longer than the average American. All that goody-goody Mormonism may just be the practices all Americans should adopt if they want to live longer and healthier lives, as the reports state that Mormons have a significantly lower incidence of many forms of cancer and heart disease. Doctors now look at the Mormon preachings as wise precautions against any number of diseases. Abstaining from alcohol, caffeine, tobacco and striving to maintain peace and harmony in their marriages and between their children leads to positive health benefits.

So the Osmonds may have the last laugh after all!—not that they would ever stoop that low. "Forgive and forget" is part of their credo.

Of course, the Osmonds are still relatively young. And it is possible that in their quest to recreate the superstardom they once enjoyed, either Donny or Marie might let their resistance be broken down—so long as nudity is not involved. Donny learned that bland cannot make it on Broadway, nor in the music industry, except for teen idols.

The suspicion still exists that Donny might have broadened his career while he was still a teen idol—if he had not thrown away his teenybopper title when he was still so young. No other star of his popularity had abdicated the throne for marriage; it was unheard of, but Donny let his heart rule his head.

It would have been easy to just get secretly engaged to Debbie, to sneak dates with her until his popularity faded with age. But that would have been dishonest both to himself and, more importantly, to Debbie. And despite his instant drop in the ratings, Donny insists he has no regrets about taking so serious a step when he was just a few short months out of his teens. "I was ready for it. Show business grew me up fast. I had a lot of responsibilities. And I was lucky in getting a wonderful woman," he says. "So I was ready for it."

The marriage and its good and bad moments have matured Donny. Certainly the tragedy that marred their first few months of marriage, when Debbie miscarried what would have been their first child, cannot be forgotten. That loss made the births of Donny Jr. and Jeremy all the more blessed to them. And that is why Debbie, for one, understands what Marie was going through and why it was important that she stay home as much as possible.

All of that new maturity undoubtedly will edge its way into Donny's new musical style. Just as his brothers went into the studio to experiment with their vocals, so is Donny back in Utah with his new group, searching for that new musical sound that will make him a star again.

Donny has also been doing some soul searching about his one-time acting career. While Jimmy, at nineteen, is vowing never to compromise his principles for a role, it is easy to do from a perch as a semiregular on "Fame." Donny does not have that luxury. That may be why he says he is looking for a movie role that is "masculine with a love story and lots of excitement."

In the same vein, the other Osmonds are looking at row upon row of doors and seeking the key that will open one of them. Because behind those doors lie the new success in television, movies, records, and theater that they still so eagerly seek.

Appendix

MARIE'S VITAL STATISTICS

Full Name: Olive Marie Osmond Craig
Nickname: Sissy
Color Hair: Dark Brown
Eyes: Dark Brown
Height: 5'5"
Birthdate: October 13, 1959
Birthplace: Ogden, Utah
Favorite Flower: Rose
Hobbies: Cooking, collects toy elephants
Married to Steve Craig

DONNY'S VITAL STATISTICS

Full Name: Donald Clark Osmond
Nickname: Corky
Color Hair: Dark Brown
Color Eyes: Dark brown
Height: 5'10"
Birthdate: December 9, 1957
Birthplace: Ogden, Utah
Favorite Color: Purple
Hobbies: Electronics, collects pianos
Married to Debra Glenn

ALAN'S VITAL STATISTICS

Full Name: Alan Ralph Osmond
Nickname: Big Al
Birthdate: June 22, 1949
Birthplace: Ogden, Utah
Color hair: Dark brown
Color Eyes: Brown
Hobby: Writing songs
Married to Suzanne Pinegar

WAYNE'S VITAL STATISTICS

Full Name: Melvin Wayne Osmond
Nickname: None
Birthdate: August 28, 1951
Birthplace: Ogden, Utah
Color hair: Dark Brown
Color Eyes: Brown
Hobby: Flying, has been a licensed pilot since the age of sixteen
Married to Kathy White

MERRILL'S VITAL STATISTICS

Full Name: Merrill Davis Osmond
Nickname: Bear
Color Hair: Light Brown
Color Eyes: Blue
Birthdate: April 30, 1953
Birthplace: Ogden, Utah
Married to Mary Carlson

JAY'S VITAL STATISTICS

Full Name: Jay Wesley Osmond
Nickname: Knuckles, Jason
Color Hair: Brown
Color Eyes: Brown
Birthdate: March 2, 1955
Birthplace: Ogden, Utah
Favorite Color: Green
Hobbies: Playing drums, golf

JIMMY'S VITAL STATISTICS

Full Name: James Arthur Osmond
Nickname: Jimbo, Little Jimmy
Color Hair: Dark blonde
Color Eyes: Blue
Favorite Color: Red and blue
Hobby: Photography
Birthdate: April 16, 1963